AND THE
PROPHETS

BOOKS BY THE SAME AUTHOR

AND THE PROPHETS

Who through faith conquered kingdoms, enforced justice
... won strength out of weakness ...
HEBREWS 11:32-34, Revised Standard Version (1946)

CLOVIS G. CHAPPELL

ABINGDON-COKESBURY PRESS

New York • *Nashville*

AND THE PROPHETS
COPYRIGHT, MCMXLVI
BY STONE & PIERCE

K

PRINTED IN THE UNITED STATES OF AMERICA

TO POLLY

LOVELIEST OF IN-LAWS
AND MOTHER OF ALL OUR GRANDBABIES

CONTENTS

I

THE PROPHETS

"Would that all the Lord's people were prophets."

NUMBERS 11:29

✠

THIS IS A CONSUMMATION DEVOUTLY TO BE WISHED. Indeed, every true child of God is in some measure a prophet. But it is of the great prophets of the Old Testament that we are thinking. I want us to seek to meet anew some of these great prophets. Naturally, such a study may seem to some rather dry, dull, and dusty. It may seem like turning aside from the vigorous life about us to look at a few fossils. It may seem at best like a ramble among ancient tombs.

Of course, such is not in reality the case. The prophets were, and are still, a dynamic group of men. They lived in days of national and international upheaval, such as our own. They heard the clash of great despotisms battling for power. They also heard the crash of these despotisms as they fell into ruins. They stood face to face then with the fact that righteousness exalteth a nation, while sin bends the neck of any people. The messages that they gave to the world were timely. They spoke to the needs of their day. Being in the truest sense timely, these messages are also timeless. The prophets, therefore, have a gripping word for your day and mine.

I

What kind of men were the prophets?

They were quite varied. No two of them were alike. Each honored his own individuality. Some of them were men of genius, while others were not so gifted. Some were backwoodsmen, while others were men of the city. Some spoke in rugged and blunt prose, while others used the language of poetry. Each saw the truth with his own eyes and spoke as he saw. But while they differed, they also had much in common.

1. They were all human. That sounds trite, I know, but it needs to be said for a variety of reasons. This is the case, in the first place, because they are men of the Bible. Many have a strange way of thinking of Bible characters as museum specimens rather than living personalities. Not only are they men of the Bible, but they were men of high character. They were saintly men. That makes them seem to some less human. In addition, they were preachers. There are those still who divide humanity into three groups: men, women, and preachers. But, in spite of this fact, so long as we think of these prophets as other than human, they will have no power to help us. Whenever any man becomes more prophet than man, he loses his usefulness.

As we study these men, therefore, we find them, in

spite of their greatness, to be possessed of many of our human frailties. Some of them were distressingly lacking in a sense of humor. That is always crippling. Some of them, I can well imagine, were a bit hard to live with. One of them, at least, was an old bachelor. That types him at once. All old bachelors are inclined to be cranky. Such are often lovely cranks, but cranks nonetheless. Some of them uttered their words of burning rebuke as if they took a kind of harsh joy in them. These preachers were all human.

2. They were all men of insight. They were possessed of the seeing eye. Naturally some saw more clearly than others, but this gift of vision characterized them all. It is significant that one of the first names given to the prophet was "the seer." It is this power to see that has characterized the true prophets through all the centuries. It is an essential part of the prophetic gift.

When Jesus was talking to the woman at the well, after he had awakened her interest in the living water, he said, "Go, call thy husband and come hither." The woman answered, "I have no husband." Jesus replied, "Thou hast well said, I have no husband: for thou hast had five husbands; and he whom thou now hast is not thy husband." Then it was that the woman looked at the Master with new and keener interest. "Sir," she said, "I perceive that thou art a prophet." Why so? Because he had looked into her very heart. He had been able to see her for what she was. He was a man of insight. This, I repeat, is a gift that is characteristic of all the prophets. They saw more clearly than their fellows. They read, as others could not, the inner facts about the lives of individuals and of their own nations and of the nations of the world.

Because of this insight these men often foretold the future. They did this with such veracity that the power to foretell came by some to be considered an essential characteristic of the prophets. But this power to foretell was, generally speaking, incidental rather than essential. The prophet could foretell the future because he understood the present. The physician who recognizes incipient cancer can tell with considerable accuracy the future of the one suffering from that disease. Even so these men, seeing the diseases from which the individuals and nations of their day were suffering, were able to foretell some of the tragedies that were ahead. These men were all men of insight.

3. The prophets were, generally speaking, lonely men. This loneliness did not grow out of the fact that they held aloof from their fellows. They were not men of the cloister. They were not men who lived their lives apart from others. They were in a peculiar sense men among men. They lived where crossed the crowded ways of life. They knew their way about the busy streets of the city. They were men often acquainted with the multitudes. What, then, was the reason for their loneliness? It was born, in part, of their insight. It was because they saw what others did not see. Seeing more clearly than others, they shared neither the faith nor the fear of the men about them. That fact put them in a class to themselves. Isaiah pictures God as telling him plainly not to fear what others feared, not to call out danger when they called out danger.

For instance, in Jeremiah's day the people were afraid not to rebel against Babylon. Jeremiah urged submission to Babylon. He saw the futility of rebellion. This caused the great prophet to be regarded as a quisling and a traitor. It put him in a class almost to himself.

Then these prophets could not trust in the confidences in which their fellows trusted. Many of their fellows looked to the future unafraid because they believed themselves the favorites of heaven. But the prophets knew that God was able, of the very stones, to raise up children to Abraham. They saw that the fact that God had greatly blessed them increased their obligation and made more sure their judgment if they failed to discharge that obligation. But the leaders of the people persistently turned from one pagan nation to another in search of an alliance that would make them secure. They were constantly leaving God out of their plans. It was the work of the prophets to remind both the leaders and those whom they were leading, or misleading, that God had a plan and that there was no salvation apart from him. Because the prophets did not fear the fears of the people, because they did not trust in the confidences of the people, they were very lonely.

4. These prophets were men of fiery earnestness. Out of their glowing souls they uttered "thoughts that breathe and words that burn." They were sure of the truth of the message they had to deliver. They had a firm conviction of its importance. They were certain that what they had to say was a matter of life and death. Because they believed, therefore, they spoke, and spoke with power. No man is

worth hearing who has ceased to believe in the importance of his own message.

So earnest were these men that they were bent on getting their message across at whatever cost. Some time ago a certain minister preached a sermon full of verbal meteors that were bright and barren. A friend was brave enough to say to him, "Why do you not use simple language that the people can understand?" But this apostle of display answered almost indignantly, "I am not going to descend to their level; they must climb to mine." He was out to save his literary style rather than to save the people. The tragic result was that he lost both. There is a power in simple, earnest effort that the man of display cannot know.

These men were so bent on getting a hearing that they sometimes resorted to means that were shocking. Take Isaiah for instance. He named one son a name that signified "Speed to the prey—hasten to the spoil"; another son he named "A remnant shall be left." His very sons were as signs to the people. Then this man, who was an aristocrat, who was at home in kings' palaces, who was perhaps the best intellect of his time, went about the streets of Jerusalem three years barefooted and half dressed. When men asked him why he dared to appear on the streets dressed, or undressed, in that shocking fashion he would reply: "This is the way you are going to look as you are led into exile unless you repent of your sins." They were men who believed their beliefs. They were men who were desperately bent on being heard. A fiery and dynamic group they were. We feel the glow of their hot hearts across the wide space of the years.

5. The prophets, as a rule, were not popular. They were generally heartily hated. It is not difficult to see why this was the case. They were too far ahead of their fellows. They were also men who dared rebuke the popular sins of their day whether those sins were practiced by prince or pauper. Being hated, they were persecuted. "Which of the prophets have not your fathers persecuted?" questioned Stephen. And Jesus said, "Blessed are ye, when men shall revile you, and persecute you. . . . Rejoice, and be exceeding glad: . . . for so persecuted they the prophets which were before you." The prophets won a place of high honor among their people, but only after they were dead; while they lived they were hated and persecuted.

6. Finally, these men had vivid religious experiences. They were all men who had met God. They were men who knew how to pray. They prayed in the finest sense, not simply by asking God for something, but also by listening to God. They were men to whom God could make known his will. They lived constantly in his fellowship. They were men who were girded and made strong by a compelling sense of mission. They were men sent of God.

II

What was their mission?

They were God's spokesmen. A prophet is one who speaks for another. When Moses was being sent on his mission, he complained that he could not speak. Then God promised that Aaron should be the prophet of his stammering brother. That is, Moses was to tell Aaron what to say. In somewhat the same fashion God spoke his message to the prophets. Thus they were able to begin their sermons by saying, "Thus saith the Lord." Ezekiel put it in these words: "Hear the word at my mouth, and give them warning from me."

This does not mean, of course, that God dictated to the prophets as one would dictate to a stenographer. Their messages are both human and divine. We speak of a bee's gathering honey, but in so speaking we are not true to the facts. All the flowers in all the world have not a single drop of honey. These flowers have a kind of nectar that the bees gather. Having gathered it, they put some part of themselves into it and lo, the miracle of honey. The prophets listened to God; but, having listened, they put something of themselves into what they heard, and we have the miracle of their messages.

It was the work of these men of insight to interpret the mind of God to the men of their day. They held the plumb line of the divine will and righteousness against the doings of men and nations. Naturally they found both the deeds and their doers crooked—out of plumb. For this reason, because they saw somewhat as God saw, they became the most caustic critics of their day. As we study these prophets, we shall see the sins against which they flamed and at which they hurled their thunderbolts. Seeing as God saw, they rebuked men for their drunkenness and their inhumanity to each other. They rebuked the rich for grinding the face of the poor.

Not only were they caustic critics, but they promised judgment. They told their own nations that they were headed toward disaster. This was the case, not because

16

God in his anger had declared that they should not live, but because, by virtue of their sin, they had ceased to be fit to live. They told great nations that were proudly dominating the world that their doom was sealed. Long since, these nations to which they spoke have passed into the night as if God said, "Depart from me, ye cursed."

Not only were the prophets the sharpest critics of their day, but they were also the ones who offered a sure hope. They saw with clear eyes the black clouds that lay along the horizon of the future, but they also saw a glint of blue sky behind the clouds. They were sure of the dawn of a better day. They were sure of this for the individual —that, though his sins were as scarlet, they should be white as snow. They were sure of it for the nations if they would only take God into their plans. Thus they warned the men of their day against impending disaster and comforted them in their hours of humiliation and over-throw. They were God's spokesmen to their day, and because they spoke to their own day, they speak to every day.

III

What did these spokesmen for God accomplish?

One would naturally think that any man who could interpret the mind of God to his generation would be the most welcome and the best loved man of his day. One would think that our bewildered and befuddled humanity would wait for such a man as watchers wait for the dawn. One would naturally expect that, when such a man came, all would give eager and earnest heed to his message. But such was not the case in that far-off day. It will never become completely the case until the glory of the Lord shall cover the earth as the waters cover the sea.

Instead of being popular men with a popular message the prophets were, as indicated above, more often the objects of blind and bitter hatred. Generally speaking, they had few friends and many enemies. For instance, when Elijah, after his brush with Ahab and Jezebel, had to seek a new boarding place, he had to go among pagans in order to find one. Earnest and courageous Amos, in spite of the sterling worth of his message, was chased out of Israel and probably died a martyr. Able and aristocratic Isaiah was heard at times with eagerness, but more often his message was set aside and ignored. Tradition tells us that he at last paid for his loyalty as God's spokesman with his life. Of all the prophets none had a more tempestuous career than Jeremiah. Once his own neighbors sought to kill him. He spent not a few days in prison and still more in hiding. In spite of the fact that he was a passionate patriot, he was regarded by some as a traitor. In spite of his tender love for his people, he was probably the most hated man of his day. He died at last in exile without one "sundown's ray of success." As a path to present popularity we cannot, therefore, always recommend the career of a prophet.

But the fact that these spokesmen for God were often hated does not mean that their ministry was a total loss. Through dark days they succeeded in keeping alive, at least for a few, a sense of a righteous and holy God who rules in the affairs of men. Though their contemporaries pushed them aside, they could not finally and fully push aside their messages. Therefore, though long dead, they still speak. This is the case because they had that to say which, both in their own day and across the years, has supremely mattered. Through long centuries these prophets have breathed upon the nations like a reviving Gulf Stream. Today they are about the most up-to-date group in all the world. Having lived their lives in times of crisis, they are especially fitted to speak to us who are a part of a world that has been turned upside down. They call aloud even now for that in our personal, national, and international relationships without which there is no hope. They call for a realization of, and a rightness with, God.

II

THE GREATEST OF ALL—MOSES

"Since then no prophet has ever appeared in Israel like Moses, with whom the Lord held converse face to face."

DEUTERONOMY 34:10 (Smith-Goodspeed)

THIS IS A TREMENDOUS ASSERTION. YET IT IS SOBER truth. Moses is the most outstanding character of the Old Testament. He is the greatest man we meet upon its pages. Among the towering prophets, who stand like lofty mountains against the sky, he is the tallest of them all. He is great in his ability. He has gifts that rank him as a genius. He is great in character. He is a great patriot and a greater saint. He is great in his achievements. As the Nile brings fertility to Egypt, so this man born upon its banks has brought enrichment to the whole world. He brought a new nation to its birth. He so taught that nation that he has succeeded in bringing every living man into his debt.

I

Look at his background. He was born in Egypt of a foreign and subjected people. Many years before his birth his ancestors, then a meager handful of nomads, had been chased into Egypt by the hounds of hunger. This weak people had been given welcome. They had been permitted to settle in that fertile part of the country called Goshen. Here they had prospered. Here they had multiplied rapidly till their few score had grown into many thousands. Then the Egyptian leaders changed their attitude toward these foreigners. Instead of continuing to be friends, they became enemies. Instead of making them welcome, as in other days, they began to persecute them.

It is not hard to see why the Egyptians took this attitude. They felt that they had at least three good reasons: In the first place, these foreigners had increased so rapidly that they threatened to become more numerous than the Egyptians themselves. In the second place, they held themselves aloof from the Egyptians. They were then, as they have generally been through all the centuries, a nation within a nation. Finally, the Egyptians feared them because of their geographical position. The land of Goshen was the most fertile part of Egypt. Not only was this true, but it was the door of entrance through which any foreign invader would have to pass in order to make war upon Egypt. In all other directions their country was protected by nature. Roy Smith in his book *It All Happened Once Before* calls attention to this fact.

If you will look at the map, you will see that Egypt is bounded on the north by the Mediterranean Sea. This made it safe from an invasion in that direction, since the vessels of that day were too frail to be a threat. It is bounded on the south by the jungle and by the rugged heights where are the once hidden sources of the Nile. It is bounded on the west by the Sahara Desert whose only inhabitants were widely scattered nomads who shifted their places of abode almost as often as did the desert sands. The only door of entry was on the east through the land of Goshen. No wonder, therefore, that the Egyptians feared to have this gate held by foreigners. Because of this fear, they decided to do something about it. Instead of going to war with them and driving them out, they decided to use them. Therefore, they reduced them to slavery and set them to doing forced labor. In addition, all boy babies were ordered exposed in order that the population might be diminished.

Now it was of parents living in bondage in a mud hut on the banks of the Nile that Moses was born. Not only was he born a slave, but he was born with the threat of death upon him. His was therefore not a promising outlook. But it is perfectly amazing what God has been able to do through some who were seemingly crushed by their heavy handicaps. Only a few years ago a man died in our Southland who had been born a slave. When he was a small boy he was traded for a broken-down race horse. But it is estimated that that small boy who seemed of such little worth, having grown to manhood, contributed by his discoveries material values to the sum of $750,000,000. He contributed yet more by his Christlike character. His name was George Washington Carver. Even so, God took this Hebrew slave and used him for no lesser task than the bringing about of the birth of a nation.

II

How did God prepare Moses for his great destiny? He sent him to four schools.

1. His first and most important training was at the hands of his father and mother in his own home. Moses had the privilege of being born of pious parents. Though these good people were slaves, they were yet in heart and conscience free. In spite of all difficulties, they had remained loyal to the God of Abraham. The mother's name, given her no doubt as a description of her character, was "Jehovah Thy-Glory."

How this brilliant boy was privileged to be trained by his own parents is one of the most thrilling stories in literature. "By faith," we read, "Moses was hid three months of his parents." In spite of the order of the king, these faithful parents believed that God had a purpose in the life of their boy. Therefore, they took a basket and lined it with pitch and prayer, put their baby in it, and hid him among the bulrushes of the Nile. Here he was watched by his sister Miriam during the day and was brought home for the night.

But this arrangement could not last. It is impossible to hide a live baby for very long. Soon he was discovered. The one who discovered him was none other than the princess herself, the daughter of Pharaoh. When wise little Miriam, who was watching, saw the princess hold out her arms to this little waif, she became sure that her helpless brother was safe. Therefore she hurried to this princess and asked eagerly if she might not get one of the Hebrew women to nurse the baby. When permission was given, she hurried away to bring her own mother. When this good woman arrived, the princess put little Moses into her arms, saying, "Take this child away, and nurse it for me, and I will give thee thy wages."

This Egyptian princess, whom we have never rightly honored, made three decisions that day that were very important. First, she decided that this gifted baby should live. Second, she decided to adopt him for her own. Third, she decided that his own mother should be his nurse and thus shape his young and tender years. This last was the decision of supreme importance. But for this, Moses would doubtless have given his loyalty to the gods of Egypt rather than to the God of Israel.

How eagerly "Jehovah-Thy-Glory" accepted her task! She felt that God had twice given Moses to her. He had given him at his birth and had given him again by the hand of this princess. But she realized that this princess' gift was to be hers only for a little while. She knew that soon he would be taken from her to live in the enervating atmosphere of the court. Therefore she knew that what she did for her son she must do quickly. Thus it was in his own consecrated home, with little of beauty except the beauty of goodness born of a vital faith in God, that Moses received his first and most important course of training.

2. Moses received his second course of training directly and indirectly at the hands of his foster mother. By virtue of the fact that he had been adopted into the royal family, he came to know the courteous and gracious life of the palace. It was also through this adoption that the best

schools and universities of the day were open to him. Thus it came to pass that Moses was not only among the best intellects of his day, but he was also one of the best educated. The record tells us that he was learned in all the wisdom of the Egyptians and was mighty in word and deed.

3. The third school to which God sent Moses was that of the wilderness. He did not go to this school altogether by his own choice. It was certainly no part of his original plan. His decision came about in this fashion: One day this brilliant young man, trained by his mother to hate injustice, trained also doubtless to hate it yet more because of what he had seen her and others suffer, went to visit his people. Here he saw an Egyptian imposing upon one of his fellow Hebrews. In hot anger Moses struck him dead. Probably, he did not intend to kill him, but when he realized what he had done, I hardly think he was sorry. He felt that the bully had asked for it. He was sure also that he had made a good beginning of his work of freeing his people. He was confident that by this deed he would win their confidence. He was sure that they would henceforth look to him as their friend and deliverer.

But in thinking thus Moses was doomed to disappointment. When he went out the next day, he found two Hebrews fighting. At once he sought to make peace between them, but the one who was doing the wrong pushed him aside with the rude question, "Who made thee a prince and a judge over us." At that Moses' fine dreams seemed to crash. How easily he was pushed aside! Who did the pushing? A nameless slave. Who was it that allowed himself to be pushed aside? Moses, the greatest man of his day.

So effectively did this slave do his work that Moses took to his heels and fled into the wilderness, where he lived for forty years.

Why did he run away? It was not, as the writer of Hebrew tells us, primarily because he feared the wrath of the king. His foster mother would doubtless have saved him from danger from that quarter. It was rather because he feared the pettiness of his own people. Yesterday, he had been sure that they were eager for freedom. He had been certain that they would respond with deep gratitude to his leadership. But now he realized that he had been mistaken. He was now convinced that as a result of their bondage they had rotted down. He saw that they had become slavish, not only in their bodies, but also in their souls. Therefore he told himself that to undertake to deliver such people would be sheer futility. Thus in disillusionment he took to his heels.

Upon leaving Egypt, Moses made his way to Midian, where he married the daughter of a certain priest named Jethro and became shepherd of his flocks. Those first days of his exile must have been lonely and bitter. We have a hint of this in the name that he gave his first-born son. It was a name that signifies "I have been a stranger in a strange land." He missed the glamour of the life of his youthful days. He missed above all else the great dreams of service to his own people that had once thrilled him. At times I am sure he hated himself for a coward. But little by little he convinced himself that the ambitions of his youth were impossible of realization. Of course his people were still in bondage, but that fact was no fault of his. It was the fault of the people themselves. He had offered his help, and that at a great cost, but they had refused to accept. Now there was nothing he could do about it.

He was now an old man. His best days had seemingly slipped through his fingers. In spite of his vast gifts and opportunities, he had little to show in return for God's great investment in him. Thus for forty years Moses had gone about his lowly task of shepherding the sheep of another man. But, in spite of appearances, these years spent in the wilderness had not been wasted. Here God had been training his servant for his great destiny. Year by year Moses had been getting better acquainted with the land through which he was one day to lead his people. Year by year, also, he had been dying more and more to his own importance.

4. The final step in Moses' preparation, one that might be regarded as a part of his wilderness experience, was his meeting with God at Mount Horeb. One day as he went about his accustomed task he saw a bush, a frail dry bit of shrubbery, that burst into a blaze and failed to go out. "I will now turn aside," he said, "and see this great sight, why the bush is not burnt." His curiosity was aroused, not by the fact that the bush was burning but by the fact that it failed to burn up and turn to ashes. As he thus turned aside, God spoke to him. It was here that Moses got a new and firmer grip of that faith that had been given him through his early training.

What did God say to him through this experience? This burning bush reminded Moses, first of all, of how he himself had once blazed against wrong. It reminded him of the hot fire of earnestness that had once glowed upon the altars of his heart. It reminded him, too, of how these fires had gone out long ago. He had now become so disillusioned that he could take as matters of course the wrongs that he was once sure could be righted. He could now tell himself that what could not be cured must be endured. It reminded him, as it may remind us, of the lost enthusiasms of his youth.

Not only did God through this bush remind Moses of a fire that had glowed and gone out, but he also led him to understand the cause. Why did Moses glow for one fiery moment, then grow cold, then fling down his purpose and run away? In other words, what was there in the bush that Moses did not possess? The answer is God. This gifted man had begun his task, in spite of much that was fine, hampered by pride and self-confidence. He had to be brought to realize that his strength was in God. By this experience he came so to learn this lesson that he became one of the most humble of men.

Finally, through this experience Moses came to realize that God had not ceased to care when he himself had given up caring. He came to see that, in the sufferings of his people, God himself was supremely concerned. "I have surely seen the affliction of my people . . . and have heard their cry; . . . I know their sorrows; and I am come down to deliver them." No Moses, however great, can deliver anyone. God must be the deliverer. But how? Here is his answer: "Come now therefore, and I will send thee unto Pharaoh." God delivers still, but he delivers now, as then, through human hands. Thus by four schools did God train Moses for his task.

III

What came of this training?

Moses, thus equipped, set out upon his mad and impossible task with nothing but a staff in his hand and a sense of the undergirding of Almighty God. Thus undergirded, he awakened his sluggish people, who had been deadened by long years of servitude.

Through the undergirding of God he led them as far as the Red Sea. Here the hopes of the success of his venture seemed utterly blotted out. The mighty Egyptian army was behind them and only the sea in front. The people were in despair. But the end of this adversity was not tragedy but triumph. The writer to the Hebrews tells the story in these words, "By faith [the Israelites] passed through the Red sea as by dry land: which the Egyptians assaying to do were drowned." This deliverance became to these people an outstanding evidence of the workings of a mighty God. It was the greatest single event in their eventful history.

But in spite of this triumph, Moses did not succeed in leading his people into the land of their hopes. When they came to what might have been their hour of triumph, through lack of faith they lost their courage. Therefore, they were condemned to forty years of wandering in the wilderness. But these were not lost years. It was during these years of wandering that Moses so trained these ignorant and petty people as to set their feet upon the road to a great destiny. He taught them that they were living under a moral order. He said, "Be sure your sin will find you out." He taught them that God was a God of justice. Through his teaching these people became the teachers of the world. It was this great prophet who made possible Isaiah, Jeremiah, and even Jesus Christ.

Let us bear in mind that this amazing leader was no accident. Surely he was a man to whom God gave vast gifts for the doing of a great work. God had a definite purpose in his life, as he has in yours and mine. But in order for God to realize that purpose, he had to have the help of a home made wholesome by a vital faith. In order for God to realize his purpose, he had to give Moses the right kind of father and mother. How amazing that this little mud hut in the slave quarters on the banks of the Nile should have been the source of such vast light and leading to his own people and to all the peoples of the world! There is no measuring what God can do through one consecrated home.

WHEN GOD CAME BACK—SAMUEL

"And the Lord appeared again in Shiloh."

I SAMUEL 3:21

THIS IS A WORD TO LIFT THE HEART AND SET THE soul to dreaming. If we can hear it without a thrill, it is either because we fail to understand or because familiarity has dulled its keen and cutting edge. God has come back. This is the great news that has passed from man to man, from home to home, and from village to village, till all Israel has been filled with a new expectancy and a new hope. The world could not ignore the return of Napoleon from Elba. The record of that return was written in terms of blood and tears. But the record of God's return is written here, as always, in terms of individual and social enrichment.

I

"The Lord appeared again in Shiloh." We can readily see what this word implies. It indicates that God had been away. "Once more the Eternal was to be seen at Shiloh,"

31

Moffatt translates it. That indicates that there had been gray days through which he had not been seen. Of course, he had never been absent. In every age he surrounds his people as the waters of the sea surround the vessel. In every age he is infinitely near. In every age he stands at the door and knocks. But so often we fail to recognize him. When we thus fail, God becomes to us as if he were distant or as if he were dead.

This absence on the part of God had stretched over a long period. It was three centuries now since the death of Moses. God had illuminated briefly a few foothill personalities during these years. But there had been no mountain peak that had approximated the height of Moses. As long as this great man lived, he had kept alive among his people a sense of God. That was a great tribute they had paid him—all the greater because it was unconscious— when they had said to Aaron, "Up, make us gods, which shall go before us; for, as for this Moses, . . . we know not what is become of him." That is, when Moses had gone, as far as they were personally concerned, God had gone. All they had seen of God they had seen in the personality of their great leader.

II

But now, God had come back. How did God come?

He came through human personality. We are made in God's image. We are made in God's image in that we are persons. We are like God in that we have power to choose, and power to know, and power to love. Since man is kin to God, God can reveal himself to him and through him.

"No man hath seen God at any time," says the author of the Fourth Gospel, "the only begotten Son, who is in the bosom of the Father, he hath declared him." To most of us God remains an abstraction until we see him in terms of personality.

It is in Jesus, the Incarnate Son, that we find our fullest revelation of God. But all the saints reveal him in some measure. The most striking fact to me, as I turn the pages of the Old Testament, is not the crudeness of some of its stories, but the clearness with which some of these ancient saints saw God. Here, for instance, is a psalm written centuries before Jesus was born. It begins like this: "The Lord is my shepherd; I shall not want." Our Lord found in this psalm such an accurate description of himself that he seems to say, "This poet was looking into my face as he sang his song. I am the Good Shepherd who giveth his life for his sheep." It is wonderful that certain great souls of the long ago saw God so clearly that they were able to be, in some fashion, a revelation of him to their fellows.

Samuel was a man of this type. He became in his own day a veritable way of the Lord along which God could walk to manifest himself to his people. Men saw something of God in him. Nor is his story by any means unique. The chances are that all of us had our first glimpse of the beauty of the Lord by looking into the face of some one of his saints. Listen to this exquisite confession of faith and love: "Intreat me not to leave thee, or to return from following after thee: for whither thou goest, I will go; and where thou lodgest, I will lodge: thy people shall be my people, and thy God my God." How had Ruth come to

33

choose the God of Naomi for her own? She did so because she had seen the beauty of the Lord in the face of the woman she loved. This, I take it, is the highest service that one soul can render to another—to bring to that soul a sure sense of God.

III

The Lord appeared again. He appeared, not in the splendors of his glory, but he appeared through Samuel. Why did he choose Samuel?

Let us face the fact at once that this choice was not a matter of favoritism. We are not all of equal ability. God gives to one two talents, and to another one. These talents are gifts. Therefore they reflect credit upon the Giver, not upon the receiver. No man deserves credit merely for receiving a gift. If you have a beautiful face, you have not yourself to thank for its beauty. Your beauty is a gift. You deserve no more credit for being handsome than your neighbor for being homely. Samuel was vastly gifted, but the Lord did not reveal himself to and through him for that reason.

Why then, I repeat, did God reveal himself to and through Samuel? It was because there was that in Samuel which made such a revelation possible. God is infinitely eager to reveal himself to every human soul. But some of us make that revelation impossible. We refuse to see. How did Samuel make it possible? We can find an adequate explanation by a glance at Samuel's background.

1. Samuel had the privilege of being cradled in the arms of a saintly mother. For years Hannah was a wife without

a child. She felt bitterly the disappointment of it. Though a favorite wife, she longed for the hug of baby arms and the kiss of baby lips. In her eagerness for motherhood she turned to God in earnest prayer. God heard her. Then one day the sweet angel of suffering came, and she held a baby in her arms. She named him Samuel, "God-asked," because he was given in answer to prayer. She said, "For this child I prayed; and the Lord hath given me my petition which I asked of him."

Having received her child from God, she believed that he was still God's child. She believed that God could do more for him and through him than she herself could do. There are some mothers and fathers who are afraid to trust their children altogether with God. Hannah was not. She not only declared that God had heard her prayer and granted her request, but she added, "Therefore also I have lent him to the Lord; as long as he liveth he shall be lent to the Lord." She dedicated her son to God. Not only so, but she dedicated him in his young and tender years.

Having thus dedicated him to her Lord, she took him to the sanctuary and put him in the care of the best man she knew, the pious priest Eli. This saintly old man was far from perfect. He had made a tragic failure in the rearing of his own sons. He had two boys who were in the priesthood, but they were a curse rather than a blessing. They, too, might have been revelations of God to men, but they missed their chance. Their failure was the fault of their father as well as of themselves. Eli, so far as the record goes, had never done a positive wrong, but he had failed to do the aggressive right. His supreme failure was in a

35

weak refusal to discipline his own sons. The first message from the Lord that Samuel had to deliver was one of doom for his pious old teacher and for his sons.

Listen to these words: "I have told him that I will judge his house for ever for the iniquity which he knoweth; because his sons made themselves vile, and he restrained them not." What a word that is for today when family discipline seems to many ridiculous, stupid, and antiquated! Yet a lack of discipline cheats the child of his happiness in the here and now. No child is happy whose will is never crossed. Not only so, but it is likely to rob him of his future. I am not now discussing how we should discipline our children. But what I am saying is that it would be better for the child never to be born than not to be trained. It was for lack of training that the sons of Eli, who might have been revelations of God, came to make religion detestable because of the ugliness of their own personal lives.

But, though Eli made a failure with his own sons, he rendered a great service to his day and to all the subsequent centuries through his training of this gifted youth, Samuel. One night, the author tells us, this winsome lad had a personal call from God. Up to this time his faith had been only an inherited faith. His religion had been a religion of hearsay. But now it became a religion of experience. God called Samuel, but the lad interpreted that call as a human voice. He thought it was only the call of Eli. His is a common blunder. There were those about Jesus who sought to explain the voice of God by saying, "It thundered." At other times we interpret as divine a voice that is of the earth earthy. Blessed is the youth who has some wise saint to interpret to him the voice of God. This ancient teacher told the lad how he might be sure of God.

"Go, lie down again," he directed, "and when you hear the voice, say, 'Speak, Lord, for thy servant heareth.'" This is a direction that is just as fresh and pertinent today as it was those long centuries ago. Eli is only saying what another said in different words: "In all thy ways acknowledge him, and he shall direct thy paths." It is as we are willing to do his will that we come to know. This is the road along which any man can walk to religious certainty. Here is a word out of the experience of one of the greatest of the saints: "I know whom I have believed, and am persuaded that he is able to keep that which I have committed unto him against that day." "I believed," writes Paul, "I committed, I know." Samuel took that road and came to know. They spoke of him in later years as the seer. He was a man who had come to see God.

IV

Look next at the services that this man who saw God rendered to his needy people.

1. During the prime of his manhood he served as a judge in Israel. His position was one of power. He was a virtual king. Under his leadership Israel found a new unity and a new freedom. As a judge he visited his people, hearing their disputes and helping them to settle their difficulties. This he did so wisely and well that no man could pick a flaw in his administration.

But, in spite of this fact, there came a day when the

people demanded a change. By this time Samuel had grown old. His hair was white. He was not quite so fit physically as he had once been. Then his sons had proved a disappointment. Further, the people wanted a king in order to be like the nations round about them. They wanted a king because they thought a king would be more theatrical and dramatic. Up to this time their government had been a theocracy, but now they wanted a monarchy. They were eager for God's representatives to be more showy, to make a greater appeal to the eye. When religion has lost its inwardness, men generally seek to make up for that loss by an outward display.

When these people whom Samuel had served so faithfully began to clamor for a change, the prophet naturally did not hear their demands with gladness. He did not wish to retire. He was not ready to superannuate. Being a man of prayer, he took the matter to the Lord. He was convinced that he was concerned only for the honor of God, but part of his concern was for himself. It is terribly easy to mistake our selfishness and wounded pride for the zeal of the Lord. God told his disappointed prophet that the people, in making their demands, were not so much rejecting the prophet as rejecting their Lord. He also told his servant to comply with their request. Thus was Samuel superannuated.

2. Then came the second, and really great, era in his life. This ungrateful treatment might have embittered a lesser man. I knew a preacher some years ago who was superannuated against his will. He became so embittered over it that he alienated his own children from the church

38

to which he had given his life. That Samuel was tempted to wash his hands of the whole business is evident from these words: "God forbid that I should sin against the Lord in ceasing to pray for you." He would never have said that if he had not been tempted to say, "All right, you do not want my services. Therefore I will not force them upon you. You have made your own bed, now you can lie on it." Samuel's Christlike magnanimity showed itself in two very definite ways.

First, in his attitude toward Saul. This young man had taken Samuel's place of rulership. The prophet could not fail to see that, though he was a giant physically, he was little better than a dwarf spiritually. How easy it would have been for him to have criticized his successor and to have made it hard for him. Instead, he became his life-long friend. When news came that Saul had departed from the Lord, it broke Samuel's heart. He cried unto the Lord all night for this backslidden king. The next morning he paid him a pastoral visit and did his best to win him back to God. Though Saul did not listen to Samuel, he believed in him as he believed in no other man.

This is evidenced by what he did in the most tragic hour of his disappointing life. When he was near the end of his journey and his doom was closing in upon him, he felt desperately the need of help that no man could give. But, having forsaken God, he knew not where to turn. At last he decided to consult a medium. Man is incurably religious. If he does not have a real religion, then he will have one that is spurious. Do not laugh at Saul's conduct as an old folk story. There are thousands of intelligent people who are following in his steps this very day. When this medium asked Saul whom he wished to consult, he said, "Bring me up Samuel." He believed in this good man in life; he believed in him in death. He never doubted his friendship though Samuel had to pronounce his doom.

In the second place, Samuel showed his greatness in that he continued to love and to serve his people. He did not look back to his enchanted yesterday and condemn the colorless today by comparison. Instead, he became so interested in the present and the future that he forgot all the slights of the past. *Life Begins at Forty* is the name of a book written some time ago. Indeed it does! It begins at fifty, sixty, even at seventy. It begins at any age that a man is willing to be shaken out of his comfortable rut and to do the task that is suited to his hands.

This wise prophet became peculiarly interested in the youth of his day. There are few surer signs that one has grown old and sour on the inside than his wholesale condemnation of youth. Because of his keen interest in youth, Samuel ceased to speak only the language of the generation into which he was born. He began also to speak the language of those of another generation. He found young men hungry for God, but too ignorant to know how to find him and how to interpret him to others. For these he established divinity schools. All the theological seminaries that have been built since that far-off day had, in a sense, their beginning here. He found a group of young men who were nothing more than howling dervishes and changed them into prophets of the Lord. Thus this man through whom God came back rendered his largest service after he had been superannuated.

Here then is a bracing word for all of us. God is the same yesterday, today, and forever. God is always seeking to reveal himself to man. He can reveal himself through the faith of a little child. He can reveal himself through the men and women who are in the stern stresses of the middle passage. He can reveal himself especially through those who have grown old and wise in his fellowship. So it was with Samuel. Therefore we are not surprised to read, "Samuel died; and all Israel . . . lamented him." Humble men and women in the most distant villages and the most obscure countrysides shed unaccustomed tears at the news of his death. For his home-going left "a lonesome place against the sky." This was the case because, as long as he lived, he brought to all who knew him a bracing sense of God. May this be the beautiful vocation of everyone reading these words!

IV

THE ONE-MAN ARMY—ELIJAH

"My father, my father, the chariot of Israel, and the horsemen thereof."

II KINGS 2:12

ELIJAH, AFTER A STERN AND TEMPESTUOUS LIFE, IS passing "to where beyond these voices there is peace." The man who knows the prophet best is privileged to witness this great scene. As he does so, he cries after his friend and master this impressive word, "My father, my father, the chariot of Israel, and the horsemen thereof." Elisha realizes that the real defender and preserver of the nation has not been an army in uniform, but a man wearing a prophet's mantle. He knows that Israel owes its supreme debt to this one-man army, Elijah. Such a word sounds extravagant, but it is sober truth.

I

Elijah was matched against a difficult and dangerous day. The religion of Israel, which has made her the teacher of the world, was in danger of being supplanted by a religion that was at once corrupt and corrupting. For a variety of reasons this danger was pressing.

First, it was dangerous because the attack that was being made against it came from within Israel itself. A very ancient phrase has crept into modern usage. That phrase is the "Trojan horse." Long ago when the Greeks were seeking to capture the city of Troy, they were unable to break its strong walls. At last they made a great wooden horse in whose bowels a handful of gallant Greeks hid themselves. Then their comrades withdrew as if they had given up the siege as hopeless. With joyful and eager hands the Trojans dragged this great toy within the city walls. Then that night while the Trojans slept, the Greeks hidden within the horse came out, unbarred the gates to their comrades, and thus destroyed the city. As long as the foes were kept without the walls, the city was safe; but as soon as they were brought within, the city was doomed.

This attack upon religion that Elijah had to fight was a Trojan-horse attack. The enemy was brought within Israel through the marriage of King Ahab to Jezebel, the daughter of Ethbaal, king of the Sidonians. King Ethbaal had not been born to the purple. He had waded through slaughter to the throne. He had won his crown by murder. Before his entrance into politics he had been a priest of Milkert, one of the Baals of that day. In this corrupt and corrupting religion this onetime priest had trained his daughter Jezebel. As a result, she took her religion so seriously that, in spite of the evil thing that it was, she boldly brought it into Israel with her. Such fidelity would have been commendable in a better cause. There are those today who, while claiming a faith that is the one hope of the world, often leave it behind when they move even from one city to another.

Now, as a worshiper of her pagan gods, Jezebel became especially dangerous to the faith of the people among whom she had come to dwell. This was true, in the first place, because of her high and powerful position. She was the queen. She had the prestige and influence that go naturally to the first lady of the land. Then she had more than influence. She had despotic power. She was, therefore, a threat to the religion of Israel because of her position.

Then Jezebel was a threat because she was an earnest propagandist. She was a fanatical preacher of her false faith. Though she possessed a religion that was so evil that it rotted its votaries, she preached that religion with an enthusiasm to which many professing Christians are utter strangers. She was not willing that her faith should be merely tolerated. She was not willing that it be just one of the religions of her adopted section. She rather seemed to have determined to make it the dominant faith of Israel.

She was a threat not only because of her fiery zeal as a propagandist, but because of her ability. She was brilliant, dashing, and strong. Something of her might is indicated by the fact that she is the most hated woman of the Bible. She is called "that cursed woman." When the writer of Revelation wants to speak of a woman at her worst, according to Moffatt's translation, he calls her "that Jezebel of a woman." This intense hatred indicates some-

44

thing of her strength. We do not hate pygmies, though we may despise them. We do not hate nonentities, though often we may look upon them with contempt. But that this woman was so greatly hated indicates something of her might. It takes a powerful personality to arouse such hot hatred.

Finally, she was a great threat to the religion of Israel, not only because she was a strong and earnest propagandist, but because she was without scruple. Carlyle reminds us that men are like the gods they serve. Since Jezebel worshiped gods that were unjust and corrupt, she naturally shared that corruption. One day, for instance, when Ahab came home in a pet because a certain peasant named Naboth had refused to sell his vineyard, Jezebel virtually asked him: "Are you a man or a mouse? What is the use of having power if you do not use it? I will get the vineyard for you." This she proceeded to do by having Naboth condemned for treason and stoned to death. Jezebel no doubt thought that she was being very tactful. This sham trial was a concession to those narrow-minded Jews whose religion had given them some sense of justice. In her own land there would not have been even a sham trial. The common man had no rights. Naboth would simply have been murdered and no questions asked.

Now with a woman like this on the throne, earnestly propagating her own religion and earnestly persecuting the true religion, it is not surprising that she met with considerable success. We can get some idea of the extent of her success by two separate utterances from the lips of Elijah himself. One of these he spoke when he was enjoying the zest of battle. It is, therefore, not colored by any sense of that depression and discouragement that he suffered a little later. "How long halt ye between two opinions?" he asked. Thus he accused his people of being crippled by indecision. Some of them perhaps had gone over to Baal altogether. Even those who had refused wholeheartedly to worship Baal were limping between two opinions. They were halfhearted and lukewarm. They were timorous foes of Baal and suspicious friends of God.

The other utterance by which he indicated Jezebel's success was made in a fit of depression. It is not, therefore, to be taken at its face value. Yet even then there was far more truth in it than exaggeration. Here it is: "The children of Israel have forsaken thy covenant, thrown down thine altars, and slain thy prophets with the sword; and I, even I only, am left; and they seek my life, to take it away." Of course, in reality this courageous prophet had not made an utter failure; neither was he entirely alone. There were yet thousands who were loyal worshipers of Jehovah. But in spite of this, Elijah could not shut his eyes to the fact that Jezebel had been such an effective foe that the cause of true religion had been in danger of complete defeat.

II

Now it was against this deadly threat that Israel's one-man army girded himself for battle. How did Elijah make his fight?

1. He made it, I am sure, after careful preparation. This I say, in spite of the fact that we know nothing of his

background. We do not see him rise. We behold him risen.
He bursts upon us like a tropical sunrise. One moment it
is dark, the next the light is flashing upon us. Who was his
father? We do not know. What mother nursed him in her
arms and breathed the faith of future battles into his
childish heart? Again, we do not know. How did he first
come to be conscious of God? When did he hear God's
call and answer, "Here am I; send me"? To these big questions we must give the same monotonous answer. We do
not know. But that he heard such call we can be sure. There
is no way of explaining this sturdy prophet except in terms
of God. He was a man raised up of the Almighty and empowered for doing battle for God in a dangerous day.

2. He was an aggressive fighter. He knew that the best
defense is an offense. It is always an evil day for any
church when it sets out merely to hold its own. No church
has ever been strong enough to dig in and stand a siege.
Churches are like trees in one respect. The moment they
cease to grow, they begin to die. A church must be aggressive or cease to be Christian. The same is true of the individual. We are born on an incline and must go either
up or down. To refuse to go up is surely to go down
whether we choose to do so or not.

Elijah knew this; therefore, he did not merely try to
wage a defensive campaign. He went at once to the attack.
Nor did he begin by flinging himself against some weak
outpost. He fired his first broadside against the very center
of evil—the throne itself. One day he won his way into
the palace and told the king and queen to their faces that it
was God and not Baal upon whom they were dependent.

47

He informed them further that God was going to turn off their water supply, that there should not be rain or dew in the coming months except at his word. Then, with the key of heaven hung to his girdle, he made a strategic retreat.

When we see the prophet again, he is still the aggressor. Once more he stands face to face with Ahab, who has had more than three years during which to nurse his rage. But Ahab does not find Elijah; Elijah finds Ahab. It is the prophet who compels Ahab to make that test on Carmel. When these false prophets are gathered, Elijah is still the aggressor. With bitter sarcasm he attacks his foes. At last he is victorious through an earnest prayer of faith that brings down fire from heaven.

On another day news came to Elijah that Ahab had murdered Naboth and had stolen his vineyard. Here again this daring prophet played the role of an aggressor. He must have realized the danger that threatened him from this unscrupulous and despotic king and queen, but instead of hiding he hurried to the vineyard in order to be there when the king came to take possession. Thus, as Ahab looked over his newly acquired lands, a shadow fell across his path. He looked up to find himself face to face with a man who was an incarnate conscience. "Hast thou found me, O mine enemy?" he asked. It is Ahab who is on the defensive. "I have found thee," came the fateful answer. Then this aggressive prophet proceeded to pronounce the king's doom. Always Elijah was an aggressive fighter.

3. He was an indignant fighter, He displayed fierce and hot anger. This was one secret of his power. We, of course, realize that our ordinary variety of anger is a dangerous

48

something. Such anger has always been fruitful of heart-ache and tears. No wonder Jesus warns against it. Yet this kind of anger, like many another vice, is a fine virtue gone wrong. There is an anger that is so worthful that God himself can approve it. There is such a thing as being righteously indignant, though it is hard to make such an assertion without provoking a smile. This is the case because, generally speaking, our anger is purely selfish. We blaze only when we are wronged or cheated of the recognition we feel that we deserve. Such anger is not righteous. It is wicked and petty.

Jesus at times became righteously angry. We read in Mark's Gospel that "he had looked round about on them with anger." Why was his anger righteous? It was not merely because it was the anger of Jesus. It was righteous in itself. It was righteous because it was born of love for another and not of mere love of self. Jesus never grew angry when he himself was slighted or wronged. That, I think, impressed impetuous Peter more than any other characteristic that he possessed. Long after Jesus had gone Peter wrote that, when he was reviled, he reviled not again. When then did he get angry? He became angry when he saw weakness imposed upon by strength, when he saw right trampled upon by might. It was in the presence of wrong done to others that his soul fairly leaped to its feet in honest anger.

Elijah knew something of this kind of anger. It was, I repeat, one secret of his power. We need such anger today. It is fine to be tolerant. To fail to be so is to fail to be Christian. But much of our so-called tolerance is not tolerance at all but indifference. How complacent we can be in the presence of such deadly foes as the liquor traffic. How seldom we rise in hot resentment when the strong take advantage of the weak, if these weak do not belong to our class or our race. There is no surer sign that one's moral nature has become flabby and honeycombed than a lost capacity for unselfish anger. Elijah possessed such capacity to a superlative degree. Hence, he made wrong to tremble in his presence.

But, while there was much that was righteous in the anger of Elijah, there was also that which was unrighteous. When Jesus became angry, it was at wrongs done to others. When he became angry, he did not seek to destroy those against whom his anger burned. Here was where Elijah's anger went wrong. He believed too much in violence. He put the false prophets to the sword. This was not entirely an act of vengeance. He felt that by so doing he was cutting out the deadly cancer that was destroying his people. But there was enough vengefulness in it to constitute, perhaps, the darkest blot upon his great character.

4. Elijah was a praying fighter. He won his greatest battles upon his knees. When James wishes to tell us what prayer is at its best, he points back to this great soul. The victories won through prayer by this man convinced James, as they ought to convince us, that the earnest, energized prayer of a righteous man is a mighty force. Elijah reminds us somewhat of the Puritan as Macaulay describes him: "He prostrated himself in the dust before his Maker, but he set his foot on the neck of his king." This prophet

was strong by nature, but the supreme secret of his might as a soldier of God was his power in prayer.

5. Finally, being a man of prayer, Elijah was a self-forgetful and sacrificial fighter. Through long years of communion with God he came to share in the divine nature. At his best, he was beautifully unselfish. He so lived and fought in the spirit of the Cross that centuries later, when Jesus on the Mount of Transfiguration, needed someone with an understanding heart with whom he might discuss the coming tragedy of Calvary, he called in conference this great prophet. Elijah lived a battling life, but in the main he fought in the spirit of the Cross.

III

What, then, was the outcome of Elijah's life? What did he accomplish?

For the people of his own day he himself felt that he had done but little. Yet he had done far more than he realized. He was reminded when his darkest day was upon him that there were yet seven thousand who were true to the God of Israel. That means that there was an indefinite number. Some of these had doubtless been won to their faith by this battling prophet. Others had caught the contagion of his courage and had stood true. In his own day, therefore, he had been to this people "as rivers of water in a dry place, as the shadow of a great rock in a weary land."

But his contribution to his own day was as a mole hill to a mountain in comparison with the service he has rendered to all the subsequent generations. He so gripped the

N.
B.

51

writers of the New Testament that they mention him more often, we are told, than any other of the prophets. In every age, to come into his presence is to feel an uplift and to receive a new sense of God. He heartens us by the sturdy way in which he met life day by day. He heartens us also by the message of his home-going. In fact, I feel like saying that "nothing in his life became him like the leaving of it."

It would be hard to find, even in the New Testament, anything finer than this last walk that he and Elisha took together: "As they still went on, and talked, . . . behold, there appeared a chariot of fire, and horses of fire, and parted them both asunder; and Elijah went up by a whirlwind into heaven."

From that inspiring scene Elisha went, not to ask that futile question, "Where is Elijah?" That question was asked by the lesser prophets who believed that Elijah was indispensable. But Elijah had taught his friend that no man is indispensable. Therefore Elisha asked not, "Where is Elijah?" but "Where is the Lord God of Elijah?" This mighty prophet has many a lesson to teach us; but none, I think, is more important than this: The need of our day is not this prophet or that prophet, this man or that man. The big need of our day, as of every day, is God. Given God, victory is possible for me, for you, for the world.

V

THE HATED PROPHET—MICAIAH

*"But I hate him; for he doth not prophesy good concern-
ing me, but evil."*

I KINGS 22:8

THESE ARE THE WORDS OF AHAB, KING OF ISRAEL. HE
is talking about one of the leading prophets of his day,
Micaiah by name. If it is true that a man is known by the
company he keeps, it is no less true that he is known by the
enemies he makes. Ahab is not the worst king that Israel
ever had, but he is bad enough for his hostility to be a
recommendation rather than a condemnation. We know
little about this hated prophet who was a contemporary of
Elijah, but the little we do know makes us long to know
him better. The man who stirred such antagonism in the
heart of Ahab must have been a good and strong man.

In calling Micaiah "The Hated Prophet," I realize that
I am using a word that fails to distinguish him sufficiently
from the other real prophets of the Old Testament. All of
these men were more or less unpopular. All of them were
hated with more or less intensity. Some of the professional
prophets managed to be quite popular. These were, gen-

erally speaking, subservient creatures who sought to say what was expected of them rather than what was true. They exercised a function akin to that of the modern fortuneteller. Sensible and sincere people, therefore, generally held them in contempt. When, for instance, Amos was accused of being a prophet, he made an indignant denial: "I am no prophet," he declared, "nor am I a member of a prophetic order." But, while all the real prophets stirred up antagonism, it is of Micaiah alone that anyone says, "I hate him."

I

How Ahab's hatred for the prophet expressed itself is evidenced from the scene before us. This is a high day in Samaria. Jehoshaphat, king of Judah, is paying Ahab, king of Israel, a visit. Ahab makes up his mind that the great opportunity which this visit offers must not be lost. He therefore reminds his brother king that it has been three years since they have had a war with Syria. He seems to imply that they have been very foolish in remaining at peace so long. They must go to war at once.

Having thus made up his mind to fight, he is not lacking for an excuse. Given the will to war, a satisfactory pretext can always be found. There was nothing new in Hitler's ability to discover some kind of paper that entitled him to attack every weak nation that he desired to conquer. Warmakers have been thus skillful through the centuries. Ahab gives his excuse in these words: "Ramoth in Gilead is ours, and we be still, and take it not."

It would seem that Jehoshaphat is just as eager to go

54

to war as Ahab; but, being a religious man, he desires to know the mind of God about the matter. He is wise enough to know that to enter upon any undertaking that is contrary to the will of God would be at once foolish and futile. Therefore, after having expressed his willingness to go, he adds: "Enquire, I pray thee, at the word of the Lord." With this suggestion Ahab is in hearty agreement. In fact, I am sure that he was expecting just such a request and had prepared for it. At once he calls in his professional subjects, some four hundred in number, and puts the question to them: "Shall I go against Ramoth-gilead to battle, or shall I forbear?"

The prophets have a ready answer: "Go up," they advise, "for the Lord shall deliver it into the hand of the king." The verdict is unanimous. There is not a single dissenting voice. Such emphatic agreement, it would seem, should have satisfied the most doubtful. But Jehoshaphat is not satisfied. There is something about this group that arouses his suspicion. He seems to realize that when four hundred men think exactly alike, they are not thinking at all, but that someone else is doing their thinking for them. Therefore, he asks Ahab a question that should have been at once a shock and an insult. "Is there not here a prophet of the Lord besides," he questions, "that we might enquire of him?" What an unreasonable question! I wonder that Ahab does not turn upon him indignantly and ask: "If we cannot believe four hundred prophets, how can we believe four hundred and one?"

But Ahab makes no such reply. Instead he gives this frank and honest answer: "There is yet one man, Micaiah the son of Imlah, by whom we may enquire of the Lord: but I hate him; for he doth not prophesy good concerning me, but evil." Thus the king of Israel confesses that he does not really believe his own prophets. He knows that they are saying simply what they have been told to say. He confesses also that he does believe that Micaiah is a true prophet. But in spite of his confidence, he makes this revealing confession: "I hate him. When I have a great function like this, I never embarrass myself by putting him on the program." Thus Ahab shows his dislike for Micaiah by refusing him an appointment.

II

Why does Ahab hate this prophet?

You will notice that the king brings against him only one accusation. He does not accuse him of being a man of bad character. He does not accuse him of being disloyal. He accuses him of refusing to prophesy good concerning him. You can see that Ahab wants Micaiah to be his own prophet rather than a prophet of the Lord. He desires that he say what is expected of him rather than what is true. In other words, Ahab desires a prophet who will agree with him even if he has to lie in order to agree. Had he put an advertisement for a prophet in the paper, it would have read like this: "Wanted—A Liar."

"How foolish!" we exclaim. Yet let us not be too quick to throw stones at Ahab. Almost all of us are akin to him. I know there is a side of us that loves the truth. If that were not the case, preaching would be in vain. There would be nothing in any of us to which the gospel could appeal.

Even in the most false, there is some love of truth. But it is equally certain that there is a love of the opposite. In short, all of us like to be lied to.

This is the case for very obvious reasons. The man who says the complimentary thing whether it is true or not is, generally speaking, pleasing because he caters to our vanity. Years ago I knew an excellent minister who had superlative skill in dealing out compliments. Sometimes I thought he went to extremes. His words would be as sweet as bonbons sopped in honey. Often he would take up from five to ten minutes before he began his sermon by telling his congregation how and why they were the greatest people that ever lived. When, therefore, a new pastor came who was not so skilled in the art of complimenting, one member made this indignant criticism: "He begins to preach as soon as he stands up in the pulpit." What a blunder!

So great is our love of being flattered that it is very hard for us to keep from being hostile to those who criticize us adversely, however richly we may deserve it. And this, let me say, is true, not simply of the pew. It is, if possible, even more true of the pulpit. Some time ago I heard a man say: "I don't care what anyone says about me just so he says it to my face." But I do; so do you; and so did he. Nobody likes to be told unpleasant things. We may profit by such a trying experience. We may remind ourselves that faithful are the wounds of a friend. We may even forgive the one who tells us unpleasant truths, but such criticism is always hard to take. It was doubly hard for Ahab because he was accustomed to being flattered all the time by everybody.

Then Ahab desires to be lied to because such lying tends to confirm him in the decision that he has already taken. Of course, he has already made up his mind to go to war regardless of whether it is right or wrong. But he is human enough to want all the prophets to agree with him, especially this rugged Micaiah in whom he has a grudging confidence. One sure road to popularity is to find out from those seeking advise just what advice is desired, then give it to them. That is one method that *How to Win Friends and Influence People* does not mention, but it is a good one nevertheless.

Finally, Ahab is eager for Micaiah to lie to him, not only to build up his ego and to confirm him in his self-chosen way, but also to make him comfortable as he takes what is probably a wrong course. The king is not absolutely sure that he is making a wise decision. It would, therefore, be a real comfort for him to be able to tell himself: "Maybe this isn't right, but Michaiah, the prophet of the Lord, says it is." But Micaiah, in spite of the king's fondness for lies, insisted on speaking what he believed to be the truth. Therefore, he got himself hated.

We realize, of course, that Ahab's hatred for the prophet is unreasonable. Why should the king hate Micaiah for telling the truth? By so doing he is assuming that the prophet makes the truth that he speaks instead of merely declaring what is true in the nature of things. If what the prophet says is false, his saying it will not make it true.

But if what he says is true, no silence or shutting of the eyes will change that truth into a lie.

Now since the prophet does not make his truth but only declares it, it is foolish to get angry with him for telling it. When the weather was very hot this summer and the thermometer stood at one hundred and two, you did not try to find relief by breaking the thermometer. You realized that the thermometer did not make the heat; it only indicated its intensity. Years ago while driving along the highway, I heard a terrific pounding inside my engine. The car came to a dead stop. I discovered that I had burned out a cylinder. I discovered further the cause for this: My oil gauge registered empty. Upon this discovery, I did not take a monkey wrench and smash the gauge. I knew it did not empty my motor; it only told me the facts about it.

A few centuries ago a certain astronomer made the daring declaration that our earth is not the center of the solar system. He affirmed that, instead of the sun's revolving about the earth, the earth is revolving about the sun. Such a declaration was an outrage. It was an insult to the scientists and a plain contradiction of the Bible. Therefore, this reckless astronomer was forced to retract. But since his declaration did not start the earth on its course round the sun, his retraction certainly did not stop it. It is the height of folly, therefore, to resent the man who tells us the truth. If what he said is true, it would still be true had he never said it. But in spite of this fact, Micaiah had made himself heartily hated by his king.

III

Now, because of the good offices of Jehoshaphat, Micaiah is to have another chance. Even yet he may win the king's favor. Ahab sends an officer to bring him to the meeting. This officer is evidently a friend to the prophet. He wishes him well. He regrets the fact that this good man has earned the king's ill will. Therefore, he urges him to say what the king desires to have said. He has some very sane and strong reasons to give for such a course.

"You ought to tell the king to go ahead with his adventure," he advises, "because that is what everybody else is doing. Why not go with the crowd? Why be a pitiful minority? If your position is called in question, you will have an answer. Simply say, 'Everybody else did as I did.'"

"But," he continues, "that is not all. You ought to agree with the king not only because everybody else agrees, but because to disagree will certainly get you into trouble. You are already in bad, but up to now the king has expressed his displeasure by merely leaving you out of things. He has not given you any calls or good appointments; but, if you continue to speak your mind, you will certainly get yourself into trouble."

Then he gives his final and most telling argument. "You ought to tell the king to carry out his plans because to tell him anything else will do no good. You know quite well that he has made up his mind to begin this war. You know he is going through with it regardless of what you or other prophets says. Therefore, why speak your mind? Is it not sensible to be silent when to speak out will do no good?"

In reply to this appeal Micaiah makes an answer that

reveals at once his fine insight and the rugged stuff of which he is made. He states what is the business of the true prophet and in a very real sense of every good man in every age. "As the Lord liveth," he declares, "what the Lord saith unto me, that will I speak." There we have it. It is not our business to agree with the crowd. It is not our business to count noses before we take a stand. It is our business to do the right as we are given to see the right, whether we stand with the multitudes or alone.

No more is it our business to stay out of trouble. Jesus had a very solid conviction that those who followed him wholeheartedly would get into trouble. So sure was he of this that he said, "Woe unto you, when all men shall speak well of you." Those who insist on the easy way never find the right way either for themselves or others. It is only as we are willing to bleed that we are able in any superlative degree to bless.

Finally, we are not to excuse ourselves from speaking by telling ourselves or allowing others to tell us that to speak will do no good. Here, for instance, is a friend to whom we should make an appeal for surrender to Christ. But we refuse and ease our conscience by telling ourselves that it would do no good. Or there is a popular evil against which we know we should make open fight, but again we allow ourselves to play the coward by telling ourselves that the evil will continue however bravely we may fight. But it is not required of us that we win our friend to Christ. All that is required of us is an honest and earnest effort. It is not required of us that we destroy any certain evil. What is required is an honest battle against it. In other words, we are not to be judged by our accomplishments, but by our faithfulness. It was not Micaiah's business to save Ahab. It was only his business to obey God. Undergirded by this conviction, the prophet was led before the king.

IV

Look at the picture. It is an impressive scene. In an open space before the gate of the city, the two kings, dressed in their robes of state, are seated, each on his throne, the one on the right and the other on the left. In the open space between are the four hundred prophets. By this time, they have worked themselves into an ecstasy. One of them, Zedekiah by name, has made himself a pair of horns by which he claims the king will press the Syrians until they are destroyed. Micaiah, I am sure, in spite of his goodness, looks the group over, both the king and his prophets, with quiet contempt. Then he says, with biting sarcasm, "Go, and prosper."

Even Ahab is not satisfied with this answer. He knows that the prophet is not speaking sincerely. Therefore, he urges him to speak the truth. Then the prophet delivers his message: "I saw all Israel scattered upon the hills, as sheep that have not a shepherd." Then he tells the king a story. The scene is laid in heaven. God is asking who will volunteer to deceive Ahab. One proposes one plan, another another. At last, one proposes to be a lying spirit in the mouth of the king's prophets. At this the Lord answers, "Go; you will win." Of course, we are not to take this story literally. God never puts a lying spirit into any man's mouth. It is Micaiah's way of telling the king that his false prophets

62

are lying to him and that his adventure will end in disaster. "I told you so," says Ahab to Jehoshaphat. "That is the way he always does." Therefore the king orders Micaiah to be locked up and fed with bread of affliction and water of affliction until he returns. Then he sets out on his adventure. But fight how he will, he is possessed by misgivings. While Jehoshaphat goes to battle wearing his royal robes, Ahab disguises himself. But his disguise fails to work. "A certain man drew a bow at the venture," says the story. Perhaps this man had only one arrow left. He put it on the string and shot at no target at all. But the arrow reached its mark in the side of Ahab. Yonder are some wild dogs lapping up blood by the Pool of Samaria. It is rich royal blood. It is the blood of Ahab. He defied the will of God and met disaster. That is the story of every man who takes his course. We do not always meet disaster in the same dramatic fashion, but we meet it nonetheless.

How about the prophet? He spoke his mind. By so doing he did not save the king. He only succeeded in getting himself locked up. But while Ahab could imprison the messenger, he could not imprison his message. While he could put the prophet in jail, he could not put in jail the truth he spoke. No more could he imprison Micaiah's character. The prison in which he lanquished has been dust for so many centuries that nobody knows where it stood. But there is one something in the ancient and ruined city of Samaria that the years have not destroyed and that is Micaiah himself. He still stands out above the ruins saying with bracing courage, "As the Lord liveth, what the Lord saith unto me, that will I speak."

VI

THE BACKWOODS PROPHET—AMOS

"And the Lord took me as I followed the flock, and the Lord said unto me, Go, prophesy unto my people Israel."

AMOS 7:15

THIS IS A PERSONAL TESTIMONY. THESE WORDS SOUND as if they might have been spoken amidst the peaceful atmosphere of an old-fashioned prayer meeting. They have about them the flavor of that intimacy that belongs to the inner circle of the saints. But, in reality, these words were not spoken to saints but to sinners. They were spoken in the heat of controversy. They are the words of a free-lance prophet who is undertaking to show his credentials to a conventional audience that is too blinded by anger to see them.

I

Look at the background of these words. The scene is the chapel— the great state church at Bethel. This church is a royal shrine. It is in a sense the king's own chapel. The priest speaks of it as belonging, not to Jehovah, but to the king. Today this royal church is thronged by many seeming worshipers. Nor are these worshipers plain ordinary

64

folks. For the most part, the congregation is composed of people who count for something economically and socially. It is a congregation that would make the heart of a worldly minister swell with pride.

The officiating priest is a man named Amaziah. He is, doubtless, a man of considerable ability and charm. He is suave, tactful, and safe. In all probability he has won his high place partly because of his gifts as a minister, but perhaps more by his gifts for ecclesiastical politics. But, be this as it may, he has so gained distinction and honor as to make him the envy of all the lesser clergy. Holding this high position, he can be trusted to look well to his office, especially to refrain from giving offense to the king who has put him where he is.

Now while this service was proceeding in a sane and conventional manner, while the rich were offering their sacrifices and bringing their abundant tithes into the storehouse, there was an interruption. A stranger stood up to speak. Perhaps none present had ever seen this stranger before. But, in spite of this fact, from the moment he began to speak every eye was fixed upon him. Everyone present listened with closest attention. This was the case in spite of the fact that he was a man of no reputation. It was the case in spite of the fact that both his brogue and his dress pronounced him a rustic.

How did this preacher compel the attention of his audience? The ability to grip an audience from the very beginning is a happy art that every speaker must covet. There are those who win attention by telling jokes, but such was not the method of this speaker. I doubt if he ever told a joke in his life. I doubt if he ever either saw or heard anything that he thought was funny. I have an idea that his lack of a sense of humor was one of his greatest defects. There are some men who never see a joke, not even when they shave. We may be sure, therefore, that this preacher did not grip his audience by his delicious humor.

Then there are those who win by dealing out a few skillful compliments. To be able to compliment wisely, tactfully, and truthfully is a very happy art. But this preacher was not skilled in this art. How then, I repeat, did he win and hold attention of his hearers? He did so by rebuking and pronouncing judgment upon their neighbors. This they felt was an indirect compliment. Israel had six different nations upon her borders, not counting Judah. All these nations she looked upon as her enemies. This prophet flew into these neighbors with refreshing vigor.

"For the three transgressions of Damascus," he cried, "and for the four, I will not turn it back." Thus he went through the list of neighbors one by one. As the prophet pronounced judgment upon those whom these people hated, their hearts grew warm toward him. We often like to hear others rebuked. We have a queer conviction that when one tears down our neighbor, he builds us up. "What a preacher!" they said one to the other. "If I could hear a sermon like that every Sabbath, I would never miss a service."

Then, just as this strange preacher had this audience "eating out of his hand," when he saw that all their defenses were down, he fetched a blow at them that at first amazed and bewildered, then left them blazing with anger. He was actually daring to tell them that for their sins the Lord was going to rise against the house of Jereboam with the sword. Shocked beyond endurance, Amaziah shouts at the speaker: "Be off to Judah and earn your living there; play the prophet there." (Moffatt)

In thus telling the prophet to earn his living in Judah, Amaziah is sneering at him. "I know you are doing this for the money. You are just another professional preacher who preaches for revenue only; but you will get nothing here, so you might as well go home." At this the blazing eyes of the speaker burned even more fiercely. In hot indignation he turned upon the conventional priest with this word: "I am no prophet, neither do I belong to a prophets' guild. I am where I am by no human appointment. The Lord took me from following after the sheep, and the Lord said unto me, Go, prophesy to my people Israel." With this the preacher may have ended his sermon in the royal chapel, but this was certainly not the end of his preaching. He has continued to proclaim his message from that day to this. Not only so, but that message seems to have become more important and pressing with the passing of the years.

II

Who was this disturbing preacher?

He was a man by the name of Amos. He was the first of the writing prophets. He, therefore, inaugurated a new era. He is known as one of the minor prophets. He is not minor, however, in the sense of being of small importance. What is minor about him has to do with the quantity of his work rather than its quality. Amos left behind him only a few glittering fragments. His sermons are little more than brief and broken outlines. Yet as brief and meager as his contribution is, so far as quantity is concerned, its quality is enormous. In fact, he said in germ regarding the subjects treated by him about all that has been said by the greatest of thinkers who have lived since his death. He is, therefore, in reality not a minor prophet at all, but one of the very greatest.

This prophet was a native of Tekoa, a little village on the edge of the wilderness, twelve miles south of Jerusalem. His was "a desolate and haggard country." It was rugged, poor, and dangerous. In this wild land Amos earned a part of his living by herding sheep. He supplemented his meager earnings by dressing sycamore trees. The sycamore of Amos' experience was not like ours. It was a tree that bore a figlike fruit. This fruit was not very palatable at its best, but was made more tasty provided it was pinched and bruised while still on the tree. Amos, therefore, earned his living by keeping sheep and by tending this rather poor fruit.

This rugged land of conflict and danger made its contribution to the prophet. Amidst its sights, sounds, and silences he learned to observe, to think, and to dream. Something of its stern strength entered into his own heart. Amos reminds me somewhat of Peter Cartwright, a pioneer prophet of our American wilderness, who was born a little more than a century and a half ago. Of course, Amos was far more able than this modern prophet. But

68

they possessed in common a rugged courage that fitted them to serve their day.

However, the fact that Amos came from the backwoods does not mean that he was backward in his thinking or in his ability. The fact that he lived in a small village does not mean he was possessed of a village mind. The easy assumption that one from a small place must have a small mind does not hold in his case any more than in that of John Bunyan or Abraham Lincoln. In spite of the fact that he lived in a village, he had a wide outlook. He had ability to the point of genius. He was also a born orator and poet. Stranger still, he was a world citizen, a genuine internationalist. Being a world citizen, he does not deal with Israel alone, but also with the nations outside of Israel. His interests were as broad as humanity.

How he came to be a world citizen, we are not definitely told. His wide outlook was due in part, I am sure, to the fact that, though living in the country, he had to go again and again to the city to sell his wool. Here he brought that fine capacity for observation that he had cultivated in the wilderness. Here, too, he met merchants and travelers from other and distant lands. Being a man of eager mind, he engaged these strangers in conversation. Trained by the silence of the wilderness, he was a good listener. By a few intelligent questions he won from them what was most worth knowing about the lands and cities from which they came.

But, above all else, Amos owed his world citizenship to his knowledge of God. Every nation in that distant day had its own gods. Israel was no exception. Jehovah was

69

the God of Israel. But Amos had come to a larger, truer faith. He had come to realize that God was the God not of Israel only, but of the whole world. He was the Lord of hosts. It was His hand that had made the Pleiades and Orion. Having thus come to know God as the God of the whole world, Amos was naturally a world citizen.

Finally, Amos was a man who was made dynamic and strong by a compelling sense of mission. As Paul did centuries later, he affirmed that he had not received either his message or his commission from man, but from the Lord Almighty. There is no accounting for this great man in any other fashion. He was not a product of his day. He was far ahead of his day. He was bracingly sure of his call from God. He could have said also with the great apostle, "Woe is unto me, if I preach not." "The lion hath roared, who will not fear? the Lord God hath spoken, who can but prophesy?" Amos, then, was a backwoods genius who was raised up of God and girded for his task by a compelling sense of mission.

III

What of the message of this man?

The message of Amos was largely one of rebuke and of judgment. In the manner of all the great prophets he spoke to the needs of his day. He rebuked those sins that he felt were making war against individual and national character. His message was therefore, timely. Being timely, it was also timeless. This is the case because, generally speaking, sin has nothing new up its sleeve.

What were some of the sins that he rebuked in that distant day?

1. Amos rebuked man's inhumanity to man. This unbrotherly cruelty expressed itself both aggressively and passively. For instance, in a day when everything was right in war, as seems the case today, this prophet rebuked the nations for their heartless cruelty to those whom they had conquered. He affirmed with solemn conviction that men of all nations were the children of God, and that God burned with hot indignation when they were treated with cruelty and injustice.

Another form that this unbrotherliness took was the exploiting of the weak and the poor by the strong and the rich. The era was one of great prosperity. Jeroboam II was on the throne. He had ruled wisely and well. The nation was becoming increasingly rich, but this wealth was falling into the hands of the few rather than of the many. The law of the land was made and administered to benefit the rich rather than the poor. If a poor man had to borrow a bit of money, or if he had to buy so much as a pair of cheap sandals on credit and could not pay, he might be sold into slavery. Amos thundered against such injustice, declaring that they were selling the righteous for silver and the poor for a pair of shoes.

Hand in hand with this aggressive cruelty and injustice went a heartless indifference. Absorbed in their own winnings and in their own schemes, the greedy grafters had no thought for the needs of others. They failed to realize that in robbing their fellows they were robbing themselves. They failed to realize that by such conduct they were tearing the very foundation from under the nation. He rebukes them for

> " . . . using for ointment the best of the oil—
> with never a single thought
> for the bleeding wounds of the nation." (Moffatt.)

The pressure groups of today that are solely concerned with their own selfish interests, with never a thought that they are making for the destruction of the nation of which they are a part, need to sit at the feet of Amos.

2. Along with this accumulation of wealth had come an orgy of dissipation. The grinding down of one group by another hurts the oppressed, but, generally speaking, it hurts the oppressors even more. These oppressors were destroying themselves by their intemperance. The prophet accused them of lolling on ivory couches while they lapped up bowls of wine. He pictures the women of the day as aggressors both in grafting and in drinking. It is always possible to gauge the morals of an age by those of the women. The morals of the women of that day were low. Amos calls them "cows of Bashan" and pictures them as urging their husbands to join them in a drinking bout.

3. A third sin that Amos rebuked was that of self-sufficient pride. As a nation, I repeat, Israel was prosperous. Wealth was accumulating, even if men were decaying. Success is always a heady wine. Many are intoxicated by it. So it was with the men of this day. "Have we not made horns for ourselves," they asked in arrogant pride. By this they meant that they had grown strong through their own abilities. They were thus sure of themselves. They were

quite certain that, if God had not made the world, they would have made it. They were drunk on their own achievements.

Along with this pride of prosperity and success there was a swelling pride of race. They were the people. God had chosen them not because of his own goodness and mercy, but because of their goodness. Against such silly pride, Amos breaks forth in honest anger. "What are you more than Ethiopians?" he asks (Moffatt). "God made them just as he made you. It is true you have had the advantages that they have not had, but that is not because of any goodness on your part. Nor does this mean privilege only, it also means obligation. You only have I known of all the families of the earth: therefore, I will punish you for all your iniquities."

4. Finally Amos rebuked his people for their blindness. The religion of Moses had taught them that God was a God of righteousness, but they had convinced themselves that God was interested in ritual rather than in right living. They were stupid enough to think that they could buy God off by their ceremonies. They thought they could bribe the Almighty by sharing with him their ill-gotten gains. Jesus thundered against this stupid wickedness in his own day. He knew certain men who robbed widows' houses and then sought to atone for their rascality by making long prayers. But he made it plain that such mingling of wickedness and worship would not avail, but would bring only the greater condemnation.

I am told that over the door of a certain saloon in Chicago is this beautiful prayer, "God Bless America." What stark blasphemy! What this saloonkeeper is saying to God is this: "You bless America while I help to damn it." Such mingling of wickedness and worship is an insult to God and man. God can bless America only as America walks in his way. While Israel was presuming on the blessings of God, the storm that was to overwhelm her was less than a quarter of a century away. Amos was affirming then what history has proved—that not only the soul but the nation that sinneth shall die.

IV

While the message of Amos is mainly one of rebuke and judgment, it does have a brighter side. Though this prophet is generally harsh and stern, he does strike a note of tenderness and pity. He also offers a gleam of hope, I am aware that certain scholars are of the opinion that some of the most hopeful words that we find in this book have been added by another. But, even if this is true, Amos still offers a boundless hope to his hearers. He offers such hope to those who hear him today.

"Seek ye me," he pleads on behalf of his God. "Seek ye me, and ye shall live." By this he means to say, "In spite of your sins, there is even yet life to be had for the taking, if you will only seek God." It is the same appeal that another prophet made many years later. "Turn ye, turn ye . . . ; for why will ye die, O House of Israel?" But if this seeking is to avail, it must go far deeper than mere ritual. Any seeking, to be of value, must be like that urged by John the Baptist when he said, "Bring forth . . . fruits meet for repentance." The repentance for which

Amos pleads and which God demands is a repentance that leads to right conduct. It must issue in right living. "Let justice roll down as waters, and righteousness as a mighty stream," the prophet pleads. Thus seeking God by turning from their sins and by doing his will, the people would find life. That was true then. It is true today.

VII

THE BETRAYED HUSBAND—HOSEA

"Love I desire, not sacrifice."

HOSEA 6:6 (Moffatt)

MY STORY IS ONE OF THE MOST PATHETIC EVER TOLD. IT might be called "A Tragedy of the Parsonage." It is the story of a prophet's broken home and of a prophet's broken heart. If it is true that all the world loves a lover, then this prophet must be held very dear. The guise in which this tragedy came upon Hosea was about the worst possible. It came through the unfaithfulness of his wife. Gomer might have been one of the happiest women in Samaria. To her much was given, and from her much was naturally to be expected. But she turned aside from the possible paradise that was open to her to fling herself into a pigsty.

I

The scene of this pathetic drama is laid in the city of Samaria. It took place sometime between 750 and 735 B.C. Jeroboam II was then on the throne of Israel. The era was one of great prosperity. Eras of depression are very trying, but eras of prosperity are often far more disastrous. For one man who can stand prosperity there are perhaps a hundred who can stand adversity. During this prosperous era ghastly abuses sprang up. The rich grew richer at the expense of the poor. Vice and debauchery were everywhere. Even some who were priests disgraced their profession by becoming gangsters. The relationship between the sexes was hideously and notoriously bad. If the people had grown rich in these things, they had become disastrously poverty stricken in those values that last.

Some ten years before, the prophet Amos had thundered against the sins of Israel in tones that awe the heart. He was a prophet of judgment. Hosea took up the message where Amos had left off. As he preached he heard constantly the rumblings of a nation that was falling into ruins. He realized that nothing but repentance could save the people politically that had become rotten in its inner life. But, while he spoke with fiery fierceness, he also spoke with tenderness. There was a note of loving appeal in his voice to which the older prophet Amos was a stranger.

In spite of the tumult of these tempestuous days Hosea met, loved, and married a young woman named Gomer. She was in, and doubtless of, the gay and easygoing social life of her time. Hosea brought to this romance the unsquandered treasure of a strong man's heart. He had never sacrificed upon the wayside altar. He therefore had much to give. Gomer in all probability was at first swept off her feet by the attention of this young man of genius who had the heart of a hero, the passion of a

77

poet, and the zeal of a saint. At any rate, she consented to become his wife.

Now it is only a truism to say that a man generally finds his heaven or his hell in the woman that he marries. The same is, of course, true of the woman. Hosea did not find his heaven. He found his hell. Perhaps he did not have as much time to give to his pleasure-loving young wife as he should have had. He was deeply engaged in an effort to save his nation. He knew that the "Indian summer" of prosperity had come for his people and that, therefore, winter could not be far away. He was certain that Assyria, was on the point of setting her war chariots in motion. Therefore, he had to give his days and nights to the calling of his people to repentance in an effort to avert disaster.

Meantime Gomer did not share the purposes of her too patriotic and religious husband. She doubtless felt herself neglected. At times she perhaps threw it into his face with petulant tears that he cared more for his preaching than he did for her. She began to tell herself, and to allow others to tell her, that she was being made a martyr. Martyrs who are conscious of their martyrdom are always burdens grievous to be borne. More and more she gave herself to the gay life of her time. Therefore, Hosea often lay awake at night longer than was good for him. Often he went about his task with an even heavier burden than that of his decaying nation resting upon his heart.

Then one day an event took place that brought the prophet great joy and renewed hope. The sweet angel of suffering came to his house, and he held his first-born in his arms. He named him Jezreel. It was the name of an ancient battlefield. Now he thought: "This little boy will bring us closer together. This baby will lay one hand on my heart and one on that of Gomer, and we shall understand each other better and love each other more because of him." But here again he was doomed to disappointment. Gomer did not become less wayward but more so. Now and then she would weep her shallow repentance on his shoulder, but always would end by going back to her old life.

Thus tempestuous years slipped by until two other children were born into that troubled home, the one a girl, the other a boy. The girl he named "Unpitied" or "Unloved." The boy he named "No-Kin-of-Mine." We can see that he named these children in bitterness and brokenness of heart. That was the case because by that time, clean-minded though he was, he had become possessed by a suspicion that amounted to a damning certainty that his wife was unfaithful to him and that the children born in his home were not his own.

But even yet he did not divorce Gomer. That was no doubt a source of scornful amazement to his enemies and of grief to his friends. Then one day another blow fell. He came home to find the children alone in the nursery. Their mother had gone. Perhaps she had left a brief tablet telling him not to follow her, that she had gone away to live her own life. Thus was the prophet's home broken up. We can picture him as he put the children to bed that night, his first night alone. He must be father and mother both now. He hears their childish prayers; then they fall asleep. But there is no sleep for him. He watches in bitter-

79

ness through the night. Thus this night passed, and many nights—nights in which there were no stars and days without sunshine. At last, as he looked back he saw God's hand in it all. Thus his very tears became a telescope through which he saw deeper into the heart of God than any other man in the Old Testament.

II

What did God teach Hosea through this sordid tragedy?

1. Hosea discovered the true nature of sin and of goodness. As he grieved over his own tragedy, he realized that, as Gomer had deserted him, so Israel, the bride of Jehovah, had deserted her Husband. He came to realize what was fundamentally wrong in the conduct of Gomer as in that of Israel. The wickedness of Gomer was not simply in the fact that she left him for another. That was only the result of her being inwardly wrong. Why did Gomer prove unfaithful? Because she no longer cared, because she had ceased to love. She no longer had confidence in the power of her husband to bring her happiness. She had become inwardly disloyal. Thus Hosea discovered that sin in its very essence is not an outward act. It is a rottenness of the inner life.

Why did the prodigal leave home? He did not leave because he wanted to grieve his father or to wreck himself. He left because he wanted to be independent of his father. He left because he no longer trusted his father's power to give him what was essential to his highest happiness. He left in order to do as he pleased. This, I repeat, is sin in its very essence. Self-pleasing does not always lead to the gutter. It may lead to a position of influence and honor. But the important something is not the different goals to which it leads but the common motive of self-pleasing that lies back of both goals.

Just as sin in its essence is of the heart, a rottenness of the inner life, so true religion in its essence is the opposite. What was Hosea asking of Gomer? He was asking far more than that she be a good housekeeper. He was asking something of what God was asking of Israel and is asking of you and me. What is that? Not offerings, first of all, not sacrifices, but love. "Love I desire, not sacrifice" is true at once of Hosea and of his Lord. "Son, give me thine heart." If God gets our love, our wills, he gets everything. If he misses that, he gets nothing. True religion, therefore, is a thing of the heart. It gives expression to itself in a multitude of ways. But the first call of God is neither for our money, nor our service, nor our prayers. It is for the giving of ourselves. This Hosea discovered through his own bitter sorrow.

2. A second discovery that Hosea made through this tragedy was that God is a suffering God. It is impossible to overestimate what an amazing discovery that was. I dare say there was not another individual in the world at that time who had made it. All the peoples about Israel had their gods. But they never thought of these gods in terms of suffering. Any God who was capable of suffering would have been regarded as very ungodlike. Of course, thanks to the gospel of Jesus Christ, we have come to think of suffering as an essential attribute of the divine nature.

But that this should have been discovered by Hosea in that distant day is an amazing miracle.

How did he come to this discovery? As he watched Gomer go from bad to worse, he tried to forget her but could not. In spite of her waywardness this was his hell, that he loved her still. Because he loved her, he could not without suffering see her make havoc of her life. It is always dangerous to love. This is the case because, if the object of our love goes wrong, we cannot fail to suffer as a result of that wrong. It was as Hosea thus suffered that he came to say to himself: "If I suffer because of the waywardness of Gomer, God, who is infinitely more loving than I, must also suffer in the waywardness of his people. Not only so, but God's pain is as much greater than my pain as he is greater than I."

It is a fact that we can measure the rise of any creature in the scale of being by its capacity for pain. A crab, for instance, is of such low order that one crab can enjoy dining off a second crab while a third is devouring the first. But as we rise in the scale, that rise is marked by a keener sensitiveness. I remember as a boy watching the bluff birds building their nests on the lowhanging cliffs above the Buffalo River. These nests seemed safe enough then; but by and by, when the river rose, they were swept away. I have watched the mother birds as they looked out from their homes of mud in fear for their young. Then I have seen the brackish water touch the little huts and make them melt. I have watched the mother bird as she fluttered over her drowning young with screams of dismay. I have an idea she was suffering in their suffering.

Some time ago it was my painful duty to bury a certain young man who had led an unusually wild and wayward life. He had been especially cruel to his mother. Finding it impossible to utter any word of eulogy, I merely read the ritual and prayed. To my sorrow I saw that the mother took notice of this. Feeling that something ought to be said, she took it upon her self. I heard her sob through lips white with pain: "He was always good to his mother." Well, he was not, but this mother was suffering. Her pain, I take it, was as much greater than that of the mother bird as she herself was greater. Even so, God's pain is as much greater than our pain as he is greater than we. In the Cross we see something of that pain, but the Cross is not a single episode in the life of God. It is what he is suffering from everlasting to everlasting for the sins of his people.

3. Finally, through this experience Hosea came to a discovery of the amazing mercy and the forgiving love of God. As he brooded over his own tragedy, he realized that Israel had been unfaithful to her Lord as Gomer had been unfaithful to him. Yet God has never ceased to love and to be eager to forgive. "How shall I give thee up, Ephraim?" is God's plea. Thus, taught of God, Hosea became forgiving almost beyond belief. In spite of the hot anger that sometimes burned in his heart, he could never bring himself to break utterly with his estranged wife. Daily and nightly on her wandering way poured a mourner's tears. He was ready at any time to forgive and forget. I think, too, it is safe to say that the knowledge of his own

willingness to forgive helped him to believe the more firm-
ly in God's eagerness to forgive. For if he himself was
eager, how much more is he whose love is infinite.

Then one day his sharpest test came as the final blow
fell. News was brought that the man who had won Gomer
from him had tired of her. Not only so, but he had sold
her into slavery. What a tragic ending for one who had set
out with such glamourous hopes for freedom! What was
Gomer after? She was bent on living her own life. She
was not going to be held in check by any regard for either
God or man. She was going to be free. But to seek freedom through the violation of law is always to end in slavery. But to seek life by the killing of one's better self can
result in nothing but death.

III

What did Hosea do now that Gomer had reached the
depths? He still refused to divorce her. Little wonder that
people said of him:

> "A prophet is a crazy fool,
> A man inspired is a man insane."
>   (Hosea 9:7—Moffatt.)

Instead of casting her off he went down into the slave
market and bought her for a meager sum and led her back
to his home once more. How did it all end? We do not
know. Here the author drops the curtain. Gomer may have
softened under such unbelievable love. She may have become a good woman. Again she may have resisted that love

and have died as she had lived. Though love is the mightiest something in the world, we can resist it. We can resist human love, even that as boundless and clinging as the love of this young prophet. We can even resist the love of God.

Before the devotion of this great and tender heart we stand amazed. Personally, I do not see how anyone could love so deeply. It is surely one of the most marvellous love stories ever written. But there is one that surpasses it. That is the story of One who came to share our lot and to deliver us from our bondage. He bought us back not for silver or barley, but at the price of life laid down. "He was wounded for our transgressions, he was bruised for our iniquities: the chastisement of our peace was upon him; and with his stripes we are healed." We may resist even that love; but we may yield to it, let it soften our hearts and win us back to God. The decision is up to us.

Somewhere I read this story. A wealthy man from Chicago was spending a few months in the bluegrass country of Kentucky. Here he met and loved a charming girl who became his wife. After marriage they took up their residence in a palatial home in the city of Chicago, where they lived together for three beautiful years. Then one day during a terrible paroxysm of pain the young wife lost her mind. At her best she was a bit demented. At her worst she was a raving maniac. Sometimes the neighbors could hear her wild screams in the night. Some complained; so the husband went to another part of the city where he built a house at the center of a vacant lot, put an iron fence around it and moved there with his beautiful and demented wife. But again there were complaints until everybody said: "You will have to put your wife in an institution." But this the husband refused to do.

At last the family physician said: "Maybe if you took Helen back to the scenes of her childhood, they might speak to her and she might become herself once more." So he took her back to Kentucky. He led her like a little child out into the old-fashioned garden and down to the river where the first cowslips and violets of spring were blooming. But as the husband watched with hopeful eagerness, there was that same wild look in her eyes. At last, broken in heart and hope, he brought her home again. As he lifted her out of the car and carried her into the house, he felt her head drop on his shoulder. When he laid her down on her own bed, he noticed she was asleep. It was the first natural sleep that she had had for weeks. Fearing that he might wake her, he watched in silence from seven to eight, from eight to nine, and through the night. At last the sunrise looked through the window and lighted her beautiful face. For an instant her eyelids quivered and a smile played across her face. Then she opened her eyes and looked at her husband, and he saw that she was her sweet self once more. "My dear," she said, "I have been on a long journey, a long, long journey. Where have you been?" That brave heart speaking out of the memory of those desperate hours and weeks and months of watching answered back: "I've just been waiting for you."

That is God's attitude from age to age. Even now he is waiting for you and me to respond to his love with a wholehearted devotion. May we make that response at this moment!

VIII

THE MAKING OF A MINISTER
—ISAIAH

"I saw the Lord."

ISAIAH 6:1

I SAW THE LORD." THIS WORD IS AUTOBIOGRAPHICAL. Isaiah is not preaching. He is not theorizing. He is not even giving us the questionable benefit of his wishful thinking. He is witnessing. He is explaining how he came to be the man that he is. It was my privilege to spend my boyhood and youth in a home overlooking the Buffalo River, one of the most beautiful streams that sings its silvery way to the sea. Naturally it was a thrill to me to visit recently the sources of this stream that I have known and loved for over half a century. But how vastly more thrilling to see, as we do here, the source of a life like Isaiah's, which was, and still is, "as rivers of water in a dry place." There is no explaining this great prophet, social reformer, statesman, minister of God, apart from this vision.

I

Look first at the vision itself.

"I saw the Lord." That is an exciting declaration. One

must needs be listless to an alarming degree not to be stirred by it. It tells of a realization that is the yearning of every heart. Consciously or unconsciously, every man longs to see God. "Lord, show us the Father," a friend of Jesus prayed in the long ago. That is in a profound sense a universal prayer. That longing has sobbed its way through all the centuries. It is older than civilization. It is as old as man. It is the very mother of religion.

"I saw the Lord." This declaration heartens us because it makes us at least dimly hope that we too may have that transforming vision. Our hope grows the stronger when we realize that the vision that was the privilege of this great prophet is by no means unique. It has been the experience of multitudes. Men of genius have been transformed by it. It has also been the experience of countless thousands of ordinary men and women like ourselves. I am thinking of some even now whose faces, radiant with an inner light, bear witness to the fact that they too have seen the Lord.

Now coming thus to see God, the prophet learned something of his character. We are not to understand, of course, that Isaiah learned all that he ever knew of God through this vision. His, as ours must be, was a growing vision. When Paul had a similar experience on the road from Jerusalem to Damascus, the Lord said to him: "I have appeared unto thee for this purpose, to make thee a minister and a witness both of these things which thou hast seen, and of those things in the which I will appear unto thee." If Paul had simply tried to cling to "these things" and had refused to pass on to "those things," his vision would likely either have vanished altogether or have become so vague and dim and shadowy as to be of little worth. We are born both physically and spiritually on an incline. We must either go up or go down. This vision then was only the beginning of Isaiah's knowledge of God.

"I saw the Lord." Isaiah's vision was, of course, not physical but spiritual. He saw God as one infinitely holy. He was holy not simply in the sense that he was set apart high and lifted up, but in that he was perfectly pure. He was one so pure that in his presence the holiest of angels must veil their faces in reverent awe and humility. He was a God who, being thus holy, seeks for and demands holiness on the part of his children. He would not, and could not, accept ritual as a substitute for righteousness. No amount of praying could take the place of ceasing to do evil and learning to do well.

Not only did Isaiah realize that God is a God of infinite holiness. He also saw him as a God enthroned. This holy God is King, not simply of the prophet's own little nation, but of the nations of the world. All other kings are, beside him, petty pretenders. God alone is King, and his glory fills the whole earth. He is not a King who is merely destined to reign, but who is reigning in the here and now. This prophet could have joined his voice with the psalmists who sang, "The Lord reigneth; let the people tremble." "The Lord reigneth; let the earth rejoice." Isaiah then came to the bracing realization that an infinite, holy, and just God is upon the throne of the nations and of the universe.

II

How did this young genius come by his vision?

Isaiah did not come to see God simply because he was vastly gifted. He did not see him as a mere matter of chance or because he was the son of good fortune. He walked to this vision over a road that our blundering feet may also travel. What God did for him he is eager to do for us. Even now his eyes are going to and fro throughout the whole earth to show himself strong in our behalf. Even now he is standing at the door of our hearts and knocking. Even now he is infinitely more eager to reveal himself to us than we are to see him and know him. How then, I repeat, did Isaiah come to see God?

1. First, God was able to get his attention. The only reason that Isaiah did not find God and was not found of God sooner was that he was preoccupied. He was not looking in God's direction. Sometimes we fail to see God because we are too preoccupied with our difficulties. Even when we pray we often look only at our needs with hardly a glance in the direction of him who is able to supply our needs. When Simon Peter undertook to do the impossible by walking on the water, he succeeded for a while. But when he became obsessed by his difficulties, he took his eyes off Jesus and at once began to sink. He was too preoccupied by his difficulties to keep his bracing vision of his Lord.

As Simon was preoccupied by his difficulties, even so Isaiah, it would seem, had up to this experience been preoccupied by his advantages. As an earnest young patriot he had rejoiced in his great king, Uzziah, who had ruled more successfully than any other king since David. To this leader Isaiah gave his entire confidence. In fact, he was so sure of the sufficiency of this visible king that he felt little need for the King Invisible. The tragedy of this was not in the fact that Uzziah was a genuinely bad man. He was not. The tragedy of the man with the muck rake in Bunyan's story was not that the straw that he was raking was not good straw. It may have been of the very best. But the fact of damning significance was that he was so preoccupied by this straw that he had no time to lift his eyes to the angel poised above him who was waiting to put a crown upon his brow. Isaiah's gaze was so fixed on *a* king that he failed utterly to see *the* King.

Then suddenly, like a bolt from the blue, something happened. Uzziah died. He died not in a palace but in a pest house. He died of leprosy. Thus Isaiah, stunned and all but crushed, became a seeker after God. In seeking him he turned to the place where he felt he would have the best possible chance of finding him. He went to church. When certain friends of Jesus came in the long ago to report to despairing Thomas that they had in a recent meeting seen their risen Lord, he flatly refused to believe them. He declared that he must have proof, proof positive and brutal. He must put his finger into the print of the nails and thrust his hand into the wounded side of his Lord. Yet, as he turned away, he may have said to himself: "What Peter and John and the rest say cannot be true. It is flatly impossible. Yet they seem to believe it. Therefore, when they meet again, I am going to be there. I do not believe their report. I do not believe there will ever be a sunrise, but at the appointed hour I for one will face the east. If such a miracle does take place I am determined to see it." Thus, when his friends met again, Thomas was there to fall at his Master's feet saying: "My Lord and my God." Thus Isaiah, looking wistfully past a throne bereft of its king, saw the Lord, the King, seated upon the throne high and lifted up. He came to find God, even as we may find him, by seeking him with his whole heart.

III

What did this vision do for Isaiah?

1. It remade him. As we read his dramatic story, we realize that we are reading what might be a New Testament story of the new birth. Through this experience Isaiah passed out of death into life. Through this experience old things passed away; behold, they became new. Through this experience Isaiah became a new creation. Naturally, we do not all come to this experience as Isaiah came to his. God is a God of variety. But such a new birth is a universal necessity. There is no substitute for it. Isaiah was perhaps as clean and high-souled a young man as was alive at that time. Yet he needed to be born anew.

See how it came about. "I saw the Lord." But this vision did not make this choice young man shout. It rather made him sob. We dare not pray for a vision of God unless we are willing to have the littleness and the meanness burned out of us. Against the white background of the holy God Isaiah realized his own sinfulness and cried, "Woe is me! for I am undone; because I am a man of unclean lips."

Such poignant confessions of sin are not the fashion of

our day. We do confess after a fashion, but those confessions, generally speaking, do not burst from our lips red with shame and wet with tears. What lies back of our loss of a sense of sin? Why does a Lady Macbeth wringing her white hands and smiling, "Out, damned spot, out, I say!" leave the modern audience cold? Varied reasons might be given, but the supreme reason for our lost sense of sin is a lost sense of God. It was when that greater robber who died at the side of Jesus saw himself against the background of the man on the central cross that he declared that, though he was suffering the very pangs of hell, he was suffering justly. Seeing God, Isaiah saw himself as he was; and thus seeing himself, he realized his uncleanness. He realized and confessed his sin.

Then what? That amazing miracle took place that always takes place when in penitence we make a like confession. It is true yesterday, today, and tomorrow that "if we confess our sins, he is faithful and just to forgive us our sins, and to cleanse us from all unrighteousness." The story of this forgiveness is dramatically told. An angel flew with a live coal that he had taken with the tongs from off the altar and laid it upon the unclean lips of the penitent and said: "Your guilt is gone, your sin forgiven." (Moffatt.) John daringly tells us that it was Christ whom the prophet saw. Surely this is the language of the Word made flesh. When he walked among us, this declaration, "Thy sins are forgiven thee," was upon his lips again and again. Here then Isaiah was reborn.

2. It was through this experience that Isaiah received his mission and message. "I heard the voice of the Lord,

saying, Whom shall I send, and who will go for us?" It came home to the heart of this forgiven man that God needed him—that, having forgiven him, God had also taken him into his confidence and was willing to use him. Just how God called him we are not told. But from the context we may be sure that he called him in part through consciousness of the needs of his fellows. Isaiah realized that the men about him were unclean, as he had been— that their need was to be forgiven, even as he had been forgiven.

Then I am sure that God called Isaiah through that inner urge to help that is a universal characteristic of the twice-born.

> "I felt that Christ had given me birth
> To brother all the souls on earth." [1]

sings one of the redeemed. I have an idea that the backs of Paul and Silas were bleeding more freely when that jailer thrust them into the inner prison than they were hours later. But it was only after he had believed on the Lord Jesus Christ that he cared enough to take these suffering men and wash their stripes. Seeing the needs of his fellows and having the love of God shed abroad in his heart, Isaiah became a volunteer saying, "Here am I; send me."

What Isaiah had to say to his fellows was born largely of his own experience. He had come to know a holy God who was King over the nations of the earth. This God, being holy, must of necessity set his face against those who were bent on evil. Isaiah saw God reigning, not as a despot,

[1] John Masefield, "The Everlasting Mercy." Copyrighted by The Macmillan Company.

but reigning in the sense that no individual or group can possibly get away with any wrong deed. Sin, he saw, is self-destructive, destroying the sinner while destroying itself. He saw God also putting his infinite might at the disposal of those who will to go in his direction. He proclaimed forgiveness for those who would accept it, even to the worst. "Come now, and let us reason together . . . : though your sins be as scarlet, they shall be as white as snow."

3. Finally, here is where Isaiah received his passion and his staying power. How intensely earnest he was! We feel the warmth of his hot heart after all these years. He lived but for the ministry to which he had been called. As Paul urged upon Timothy, he gave himself wholly to it. He gave his two sons names that made them proclaimers of his message to themselves and to the men of his day. Though a blue blood and the best intellect of his time, he went about the streets of Jerusalem all but naked in his passionate earnestness to get a hearing for his message.

He was as powerful as he was passionate. There was a high courage in his heart that enabled him to face the most hopeless situations with quiet confidence. When Ahaz was almost frightened out of his wits because Rezen of Damascus and Pekah of Samaria were coming against him, Isaiah reminded him of the impotence of these kings, calling them remnants of burned-out torches. He declared that in quietness and confidence should the king find strength, but that if he failed to believe he should not be established! A yet sharper test found this prophet steadfast. When the doom of the city of Jerusalem seemed certain because of the near presence of the mighty Assyrian army, Isaiah held firm to the faith that God would save the city, and God did not let him down. Thus was he then, and even to this hour, "as the shadow of a great rock in a weary land."

IV

How came this vision to have these mighty results in the life of Isaiah?

We whose experiences have not been so dramatic are prone to the conviction that this vision was able to work its marvelous transformation in the life of Isaiah because it was so spectacular. Generally we feel the same about the experience of Paul. Here went this hothearted man on his mission of persecution. Suddenly there was a flash and a fall and the onetime persecutor was brushing the desert sands from off his knees and saying, "True is the saying, and deserving of universal acceptance, that Christ Jesus came into the world to save sinners." "Of course these men were remade," we say. "If I should have such a vision, it would remake me."

But it was not this vision in itself that remade Isaiah. Nor was it the vision in itself that remade Paul. The great apostle gives the secret of the transforming power of his vision in these words: "I was not disobedient unto the heavenly vision." Isaiah might have gone from the splendor of this vision in the temple, as Paul might have gone from the splendor of his vision in the desert, to a deeper darkness. They came into the fullness of the light through their obedience. That road is open to you and me. By living up to the best we know, we too can come to spiritual certainty.

The important question, therefore, is not how you came to this new birth but whether you really have come. I read somewhere that there is a flower in the tropics that, when it blooms, makes a report like the firing of a rifle. But that is not the way the roses bloom in my garden. I go out in the late afternoon and see a bud. The sun sets and the night baptizes that blossom with dew. The next morning the sun kisses away the dew and a rose is born. Not even the bee that was gathering nectar at the heart of that rose heard the slightest sound. Yet my rose has blossomed as genuinely as that flower that made a report like the firing of a rifle. Isaiah and Paul were born anew through a spectacular vision, but the Lord opened the heart of Lydia that she believed the word. The how of our new birth is interesting, but only the fact is essential.

IX

THAT MIGHTY MINORITY—ISAIAH

"Except the Lord of hosts had left unto us a very small remnant, we should have been as Sodom."

ISAIAH 1:9

THIS DOCTRINE OF THE REMNANT IS CENTRAL IN THE faith of Isaiah. "Remnant" is a word that all of us can understand. When I was a boy, my mother used to make a good many of the garments we wore. When the garment was made, there were usually a few remnants left. These bits of cloth were often used for the making of a new quilt or rug or rag carpet. At Thanksgiving or Christmas when we have turkey, there are usually fragments left that torment the family with hash. A remnant, then, is the minority that is left after the majority has been used or destroyed.

This idea of the remnant is not entirely original with Isaiah. Amos uses the same word, but his remnant is a dead, rather than a living, something. Those who are to escape, after the destruction of Samaria, he compares to the fragments of a lamb taken from the jaws of a lion. Nothing is left of this slaughtered lamb but a leg or a part of an ear. But Isaiah's remnant is a vital something. He takes us to a tree that has been cut down and shows us a shoot springing up from the stump of that tree. This shoot is not as large as the parent tree, but it is a living and growing something. So is Isaiah's remnant.

The prophet's faith in this remnant is so strong as to be almost an obsession. We realize this from the fact that he refers to it again and again. We realize it from the name that he gives his first-born son. Just imagine yourself back across the years on the streets of the ancient city of Jerusalem. You see Isaiah, your friend, coming toward you. He has a small boy by the hand. After you have greeted each other, the prophet says: "Let me present my son, Shear-Jashub."

"Shear-Jashub," you reply. "Is that a family name?"

"No," answers the prophet, "but it is a name that embodies my faith. It means that a remnant shall be left. I gave my boy this name to help him share my faith. I gave him this name to fortify my own soul. Every time I take a walk with him, as today, every time I see him at play, every time he calls to me day or night, I am reminded that a remnant shall be left."

Let us look, then, at the content of this faith.

I

First, this conviction of Isaiah's that a remnant should be left, while full of sunshine, was also full of shadow. If a few were to be left, then the many were to go into exile. Of this tragedy Isaiah was profoundly convinced. I think he was by nature and grace an optimist. In spite of all adverse circumstances he certainly faced the future with hope. But in spite of this he was convinced that his nation, in the main, was doomed.

How did he come by this conviction? It was born of what he knew about his own people and of what he knew about God. As to his own people, he had been forced to the conviction that in spite of their professed loyalty to God they were in reality, disloyal. They were people of unclean lips. They were people who drew near to God with their lips and honored him with their mouths while their hearts were far from him. They were a prideful people, fixing their faith upon themselves and upon their own schemes instead of upon the living God.

But the God whom they claimed to worship, the God whom Isaiah knew, was a God infinite in holiness. He was a God perfect in goodness. Being perfect in holiness and goodness, he was a God who was constantly at war with evil. He was a fiery crusader against all that is wrong. Since his own people were wrong, God was, in the very nature of things, their antagonist. In spite of all his gracious promises, in spite of his assurance that all the nations of the earth were to be blessed through their race, he was bent upon their destruction.

We can understand something of the antagonism of God against all that is evil by what we know of Jesus. Sometimes we speak of him as the gentle Galilean. Gentle he was. He was the meekest of all men, but that does not mean that he went about smiling with indiscriminate approval upon those who were good and those who were evil. There were those whom he did approve—those to whom he spoke words of commendation that thrill to this hour. But there were others whom he condemned. There were some for whom he could find no words too bitter. He called them a generation of snakes and wondered in indignation how they could escape the damnation of hell. He never held out the slightest hope of anything but utter loss to the man who persisted in his sin.

Therefore, knowing God as he did, Isaiah could not resist the heartbreaking conviction that his rebellious nation was doomed. He was sure that not only the soul that sinneth should die, but the nation as well. He was sure that, in the very nature of things, sin destroys the sinner. Not only does sin destroy the sinner, but sin destroys itself. He was sure that the strong man, in spite of his strength, should be as tow and that his sin should be as a spark and that they should burn together. We have seen that conviction vindicated in the lives of men and nations. Here is a man, for instance, who is a slave to liquor. His appetite is working his ruin. That same appetite destroys itself by destroying the sinner. It is true of the nation. However strong despotisms have grown by preying upon weaker nations, in the process of destroying others they have always destroyed themselves. Isaiah tells his own people, as he tells us, that the nation that turns from God travels surely toward ruin.

II

But while this prophet was convinced that the great majority of his people were headed for exile, he was equally sure that a remnant, a chosen few, a hopeful handful, was to be preserved. This faith was born in part of the fact that he was sure that there were still those who were loyal to God. But his supreme assurance of the survival of a chosen few was born of his faith in God.

Why was he so sure that the majority were to be destroyed? Because they had turned from God, and, in the very nature of things, God had to fight against them. In the same fashion, since God is perfect in goodness, he can walk with, and put his infinite power at the disposal of, those who are going in his direction. The same perfect goodness that makes the antagonism of God against evil a necessity makes his invincible friendship for goodness also a necessity. Isaiah, therefore, can say what the author of the Fourth Gospel said centuries later: "The light is still shining in the darkness, for the darkness has never put it out."

This conviction that God would preserve a remnant was not always easy for Isaiah to hold. It was put to the test more than once. That test reached its climax, I think, during the reign of Hezekiah. At that time there were two great world powers—Assyria in the north and Egypt in the south. Between these were smaller nations, such as the nation to which the prophet belonged, which took shelter under the wings now of one of these nations and then of the other. A few years before, in an hour of crisis, King Ahaz, in spite of the earnest protest of Isaiah, had called on Assyria for help with the result that his nation had become a vassal of Assyria. But Hezekiah joined Egypt and other nations in an effort to throw off the Assyrian yoke.

But the results were disastrous. The Assyrian army defeated Egypt and her weaker allies. Judah was at the mercy of the foe. All her cities had been taken except Jerusalem. The conqueror was then only thirty-five miles from this defenseless city. So hopeless was the outlook that Hezekiah sent a delegation to ask for terms. The conqueror demanded all the wealth of ivory, of silver, and of gold that was in the palace and the temple. But when these were given, the greedy conqueror was not satisfied. Then the king sent another delegation. These returned in tears, for the despot demanded the surrender of the city. Then an Assyrian officer came to taunt the people with their weakness. He promised them two thousand horses if they would set riders upon them. He knew that they had not that many men fit to fight in the city. Next he offered them a bribe: "Surrender, and my master will take you to another land like your own, where you can live, each under his own vine and fig tree." At last there came a letter from the conqueror himself. This was the last straw. He warned the king of the futility of his refusal to surrender. "Look," he seemed to say, "how my armies have marched over other nations and have destroyed them utterly. For what can you hope?"

It was in this hour when Hezekiah was practically desperate that he appealed to the prophet. What was the result? The faith of Isaiah that a remnant should be left stood out just as unshaken in this terrific tempest as it had done in calmer days. He told the king that he was not to be afraid. He told him that God was going to treat this conqueror as one might treat a horse or an ox. "I will put my bit in his mouth, my ring in his nose, and turn him about and he shall not come near the city." Such assurance must have seemed futile and absurd. There were nearly two hundred thousand soldiers ready for the attack. How could there be any hope of escape? Yet the attack that seemed so sure was never made. Some pestilence so decimated the army that the stragglers who were left were glad to make their escape from a land of death. Thus, while the nation was largely destroyed, it was not utterly destroyed. A remnant was left.

Now what happened here is not altogether unique. One of the miracles of the centuries has been the indestructibility of goodness. However trying the situation, however triumphant evil seems, there have always been some good men and women. In the old Genesis story, when it looked as if all mankind were rushing down the steep declivity that ended in the Flood, there were a few who continued to live because they were fit to live. God always preserves for himself a chosen few. However complete the moral disaster of any generation may seem, goodness has never been, and can never be, destroyed.

To this faith we must hold. It has been our lot to live through one of the darkest periods of human history. We have seen a nominally Christian nation become unspeakably vicious. Yet we know that even in Germany goodness was never completely destroyed. Einstein, an exile from Germany, said some years ago that he had once felt no interest in the church, but that his attitude had changed. It changed for one reason. When Hitler came to power, this great scientist looked to the universities to oppose him; but in this he was disappointed. Then he looked to the writers, but these also let him down. The one small group, he confessed, that never bowed its knee was made up of churchmen.

III

Not only was this prophet sure that a remnant should be left. He was equally sure that this remnant was the hope of the world. Isaiah was not a pessimist. In spite of his clear view of impending disaster for the many, he was an unconquerable optimist. Because he was sure of God, he was sure of the final triumph of righteousness. Even in his dark day, he foresaw a time when the waste of war would be ended, when the weapons of war would cease to be liabilities and become assets. Men would beat their swords into plowshares and their spears into pruning hooks. But this was to come to pass at the hands not of the many but of the few.

This confidence of Isaiah in the few rather than in the many has been vindicated again and again. In fact, all our progress has originated with the few, never with the many. There was a time when belief that the earth is round instead of flat was the conviction not of millions but of one. There was a time when only the smallest handful believed it possible for man to fly through the air.

In the same fashion all our social reforms have been born in the hearts of the few. There was a time when everybody accepted slavery, but by and by a few became convinced that it was an evil thing. These won others to this conviction till slavery was destroyed. One has called attention to the fact that our American colonies won their freedom, not by a mass movement, but through an intelligent and militant minority. There were about as many Tories in the colonies as revolutionists. There were also an equal number of neutrals and halfhearted folks who sided now with one group and now with another, according to the fortunes of war.

We pride ourselves in this country on the rule of the majority. But too often we are ruled by well-organized minorities. We have great American cities where everybody can vote, but where the vote when cast counts for little more than it would have counted if it had been cast in Hitler's Germany. Too often in democratic America, as in communist Russia, political power is in the hands not of the many but of the few.

But if the minority is important in discovery, in social reform, in politics, that importance reaches its climax in the realm of religion. Here, above all else, it is quality and not quantity that counts. Some were thrilled recently by a declaration, based on the Gallup poll, that ninety-nine per cent of the American people believe in God. But before we thrill over that, we had better ask what this faith in God does for those who possess it. What effect does it have on their personal lives? Is it making them the kind of men and women with whom God can walk? Is it making of them crusaders whom God can use for the bringing in of a better day?

Years ago a gallant-hearted man in a concentration camp watched Rome as she set herself to exterminate the church. This man knew the church of that day. He was conscious of its imperfections. He was conscious of the few that made up its membership. Only one tenth of one per cent of the population of the Roman Empire was Christian. Yet he staked his faith on this hopeful handful, and was not disappointed. It was this one tenth of one per cent that conquered, not the ninety-nine and nine tenths per cent. Mark you, these did not win because they were a minority, but in spite of it. No more were they right because they were a minority; but, because they were right, the victory was theirs.

What is the greatest need of our day? We need more Christians, but we need even more a better type of Christian. Two grains of corn that have vitality in them would be worth far more toward the raising of a crop than a million tons that, when planted, would not come up. One shaker of salt that has kept its savor is worth far more than a whole shipload that has become insipid. It is vitality that counts.

Today we possess a new conviction as to the importance of missions. Some of our boys who went out to far lands in wartime learned at first hand something of the worth of the missionaries. They saw their own wounded saved and nursed back to life by black men and women whose fathers were head-hunters. A writer in the *Saturday Evening Post* tells us that the one thing which has kept the respect and friendship of China for the white man has been the missionaries. These people who have made for us all round the world what Willkie called "a reservoir of good will" have been not a multitude but a small minority of vital men and women.

It is the minority that keeps open the doors of our own

church. It is not a majority but a minority that makes possible our morning services. Those who make possible the evening service are a yet smaller minority. Those who support the work of the church by their gifts are often a minority. Those who take upon themselves the doing of its work are a yet smaller minority. It is the few rather than the many who can say with Paul: "I know whom I have believed, and am persuaded that he is able to keep that which I have committed unto him against that day."

What then does this faith of Isaiah have to say to me? It ought to save me from putting my confidence in mere numbers. Bigness is not enough. It ought to save me from despising the day of small things. Last of all, this faith ought to make me more determined to be a part of that saving minority that is the hope of the world. Whatever others may do, I may be a part of the remedy rather than of the disease. However many others may throw away their chance, I can offer my life as a roadway along which Almighty God can walk for the bringing in of a better day.

X

A REASONABLE RELIGION—MICAH

"He hath shewed thee, O man, what is good; and what doth the Lord require of thee, but to do justly, and to love mercy, and to walk humbly with thy God?"

MICAH 6:8

WE KNOW VERY LITTLE ABOUT MICAH EXCEPT WHAT he tells us in his brief book. We do know that he was a member of a quartet of prophets who were contemporaries. These four men Amos, Hosea, Isaiah, and Micah probably exerted a greater influence upon religious thinking than any other four of the Old Testament. Micah, like Amos, lived in the country; but he was not a shepherd. He was a farmer. Living in the country, he was naturally a bit suspicious of the city. This suspicion soon changed into hot indignation. There was a reason for this. It was men from the city who were pillaging and plundering the small farmers whom Micah knew personally. Hence this prophet came to look upon the cities of Jerusalem and Samaria as veritable cesspools of iniquity and injustice.

As his fellow prophets, Micah was undergirded by a deep sense of mission. He felt himself called of God to denounce the evils that were blighting his people. "I am full of power by the spirit of the Lord . . . to declare unto Jacob his transgression, and to Israel his sin." But his ministry was far more than a ministry of denunciation. His message was also constructive. In fact, this man was inspired to define for us the will of God, both for the individual and for the world, with a beautiful simplicity surpassing that of any other prophet of the Old Testament. In truth, it is doubtful if any man in all the centuries that have past since that far-off day has improved on Micah's definition of real religion.

"What doth the Lord require of thee?" he asks. In other words, what is necessary to please God? In answer he passes by ritual, he passes by sacrifice, which was a fundamental part of the worship of that day, to give this simple and profound answer. "What doth the Lord require of thee, but to do justly, and to love mercy, and to walk humbly with thy God?" How beautifully simple! A child can understand it. How vastly profound! The wisest of men cannot run past it. Here is a word for every man in every age. Often religion seems a vague and unreal something. But not so is the religion of this prophet. Here is a religion that fits into life as we know it and live it.

I

What is it to do justly? Justice is fair-mindedness in action. Just conduct is the outward expression of inward honesty and sincerity. Such conduct is admired by every unwarped mind. "For justice every place a palace and all seasons summer."

This doing justly, playing the game fairly, is to cover the whole circumference of life. It is to govern our play. When boys and girls play games, they are to play fairly. Anyone who cheats in a game is likely to cheat in matters of greater importance. The same is true of an adult. A certain humorous writer declares with more truth than humor that there are few sharper tests than that which comes to a golfer when his ball is in the rough and nobody is looking on but God. Years ago I watched a hard-fought tennis match. There was a questionable decision that went in favor of the server. At once the server drove both balls into the net, and the crowd applauded. They were convinced that he was too good a sportsman to desire a point which he had not justly won.

Justice also has to do with all our business relationships. It was a lack of justice between man and man that filled Micah with such hot indignation. As he looked about him, he saw "priests pattering oracles for pay." He beheld so-called prophets who would pronounce a blessing if they were paid, but would curse if they were not. He saw judges accepting bribes. He saw the powerful rich taking such advantage of the poor peasants that he accused them of stripping the hide off their flesh. That conception has come down to us. Today we speak of getting skinned in a trade. These plunderers were going even further. They were practicing cannibalism. This they were doing, not by actually eating the flesh of their victims, but by cheating them of the goods upon which life depended.

His is a word that is needed in every age. There is a pressing need for justice between capital and labor. We are concerned that the employer pay a just wage. We are also concerned, if we are just, that the employee do a just day's work. We need fairness between buyer and seller— fairness on both sides of the counter. In fact, we are to handle the tools of our trade day by day as honestly and religiously as we handle the Communion cup on Sunday morning.

Then we are to be just in our judgments one of another. "Judge not," said Jesus, "that ye be not judged. For with what judgment ye judge, ye shall be judged; and with what measure ye mete, it shall be measured to you again." What does Jesus mean by this warning? I do not take it that he is forbidding our reaching a conclusion as to the degree of worth or of worthlessness of the men and women with whom we have to do. Such conclusions are made necessary by our Lord's next command: "Give not that, which is holy unto the dogs, neither cast ye your pearls before swine." We can follow out this command only by reaching some conclusion as to who is swinish and who is not.

What then is Jesus forbidding? He is forbidding judgments that are harsh and unfair. He is forbidding us to play the role of faultfinder. He is forbidding us to reach conclusions that have no foundation in fact. In short, he is forbidding those hasty criticisms born of ignorance or prejudice. "Judge righteous judgment," he urges. Therefore since we are so little able to know both the deeds and the motives of others, we ought to be slow to pass sentence. This is a word for the pulpit quite as much as for the pew.

There is another field for the exercise of justice that comes close to all of us. Americans have a race problem that has been considerably aggravated in recent years. Southerners are naturally resentful of the type of outside interference that seeks to erase by a wave of the hand difficulties which are the growth of centuries. But they must allow no kind of resentment to make them unfair. Justice is always needful, but it is never more needful than when we are dealing with those whom we have at a disadvantage, nor is it ever so beautiful as then.

We ought to be just to the membership of the organizations of which we are a part. One organization of supreme importance to which we belong is the home. Now I know a home needs more than justice, but it certainly cannot get along with less. How many husbands and wives separate for lack of fair play. Some will not play fair financially. Some refuse to play fair in matters more intimate and personal. The husband who takes privileges that he would not allow his wife is a cheat. Not only does he cheat his wife, but he cheats himself, his children, and society.

Parents owe it to God and man to play fair with their children. Every child has a right to be wellborn. Every child has a right not only to a mother but to a father. All parents owe their children the right sort of training. Dr. Link, a noted psychologist, tells us that children who go to Sunday school have a higher personality rating than those who do not. He tells us that children whose parents attend church have a higher personality rating than the children of parents who do not. If we play fair with our children, they are likely to play fair with us. We ought to be fair in the home.

Most of us belong to the church. I like that word "belong." It means that the church has a claim on us. It has a claim because of our own voluntary choice. We stood at its altar and took upon ourselves the solemn vows of the church. Therefore, we ought fairly to discharge these vows. We have no right to take a course that, if others should take it, would weaken, if not wreck our church.

Finally, we are to be just in our community relationships. To have a good community we must have good homes, good churches, good schools, clean places of amusement. We ought to contribute to all that helps to build a good community. As we owe a debt to the community, so we are indebted to the nation and the world. We asked some millions of our choice young men and women to venture their all during the bloody days of war. We ought to deal fairly with them now that the war is over.

Why is it the will of God that we should be just? He is asking justice at our hands because justice is a badge of character. He is eager that we be just because he wants us to be like himself. Ours is a just God. He is no respecter of persons. He always gives every man a square deal. He yearns that we be like himself.

Then he is eager for us to be just because he is more than a judge. He is a father. Being a father, he is eager that his children be just to their brothers. If one of my boys were do the other an injustice, with which one would I side? I would side with both. I would be sorry for the one who suffered the injustice. I would be more sorry still, in spite of my indignation, for the one who inflicted that injustice. No good father can fail to grieve when one child takes an unfair advantage of the other.

Finally, God is eager for us to be just because he knows what injustice will do to all human relationships. To build on injustice is to build on a time bomb, which sooner or later will explode and blow the superstructure into bits. This will be the case regardless of the skill, care, and expense with which we may have builded it. It remains forever true that there can be no permanent social order, no lasting organization of any kind, that is not founded upon justice. No wonder, therefore, our Lord is asking that we be just, one toward another.

II

God asks not only that we be just, but also that we be kind. If justice is fair-minded in action, kindness is something better still. It is love in action. Kindness is a child of love. "Love suffereth long, and is kind." Merely to be kind does not sound so very heroic, yet nothing would do more to sweeten life and to change human desert into garden than plain, everyday kindness.

Kindness is also Godlike. Our God is infinitely kind. This the Bible tells us again and again. But we receive our greatest assurance of God's kindness in that he is like Jesus. And how kind was our Lord! Luke sums up his life in a single beautiful sentence by saying that he went about doing good. That is just another way of saying that he went about being kind.

One day Jesus told the story of a man whom the whole world had agreed to call good. Why have all men in every age reached the same decision with regard to this Samaritan? We have only one view of his face, one single snapshot. But this shows him in what we regard as a typical pose. In this one picture he is doing an act of kindness; hence we call him good. But the fact that kindness is always good does not mean that it is goody-goody. Kindness sometimes has to wound. When a surgeon is called to see a patient with an acute attack of appendicitis, the easiest way out might be repeated shots of morphine. But out of real kindness he resorts to the knife. Kindness, whether its face seems harsh or gentle, is always love in action.

The field for the exercise of kindness is everywhere. There is seldom a day so uneventful that we do not have an opportunity to employ it. Kindness is needed everywhere. But the closer our relationships to each other, the more it is needed. We come closer together in the home than anywhere else; therefore, there is no better place for the practicing of kindness than among the folks with whom we have to live day by day. Yet, I have known a few people who were more kindly and gracious everywhere else than in their own homes. Kindness enriches both the giver and the receiver. It makes living together easier. It saves from what is often the sharpest pang of separation when the one we love reaches the end of the journey. It was my painful duty to conduct a funeral sometime ago where the grief of the bereaved was unusually bitter. I knew the situation well enough to be confident that the sharpest pain of that grief grew out of the memory of unkindness.

Kindness is a great luxury. But it is far more than a luxury, it is a necessity. Jesus told the story of a certain rich man who lifted up his eyes in hades. This was the case not because he had committed a crime. It was the case because he had not had enough kindness to make him willing to help a beggar who lay at his very gate. In the picture that Jesus gave of the final judgment, there were some who received no welcome but were turned away. Why? They were so devoid of kindness that their presence would have changed any kind of heaven into a hell. No place can be heavenly where hearts are unkind. But there were others who were made welcome. This was the case because they were so full of "the milk of human kindness" that, had they been sent into hell, they would have changed it into heaven. Kindness is a necessity.

III

"What doth the Lord require of thee, but to do justly, and to love mercy, and walk humbly with thy God?"

It is this walking with God that to some will seem unnecessary and unreal. To be just and kind, is not that enough? That is a religion that the man of the street feels he can get his teeth into. But walking with God, why is that necessary? Why does God will that for us?

1. God yearns for us to walk with him because we are the children of his love. Therefore, he is so eager for our fellowship that no gift we can possibly make him can be a substitute for the gift of ourselves. God so longs for our

companionship that he is willing to bear any cross in order to win it. The shepherd who found that one sheep was missing could not be satisfied. He braved the dangers of the wild in order to find it. God is like that. He seeks not ours but us.

2. God longs for our fellowship not only because he cannot be satisfied without us, but because he knows that we can never be satisfied without him. Every man is possessed of a hunger for God that nothing else can satisfy. It is true that we often do not know what it is for which we are hungering and thirsting. Yet this remains, that there is no true satisfaction for any human soul except in the fellowship of God.

Finally, God longs for our fellowship because he knows that it is only as we walk with him that we shall be really just and kind. Here is a lovely little brook. It is singing its way to the sea. "There is something worth while," I say as I look at it. "It is a poem of usefulness and beauty. But the spring far up yonder among the rugged hills, I care nothing about at all." Yet unless we have the spring we cannot have the lovely stream that flows from it. Justice and kindness at their best flow out of this lovely spring of fellowship with God. When this fellowship is broken, the stream is likely to dry up.

What then ought to be my resolution for today? I ought to resolve to be just and kind and to live in fellowship with God. I can do nothing less than this and be a real Christian. I can do nothing bigger than this, however great my gifts. I can begin in the here and now by an inward dedication to my Lord. I ought to do this in the realization that the closer I get to God, the more just and kind I shall become. The more just and kind I become, the closer will be my fellowship with God. I can make no higher resolution than this.

XI

THE RELUCTANT PROPHET
—JEREMIAH

*"Alas, my mother! you have borne me
to clash and quarrel with all the world!"*

JEREMIAH 15:10 (Moffatt)

JEREMIAH WAS A MAN OF SUBSTANCE, AS IS EVIDENCED
by his ability to buy land and pay for it. He belonged
to the nobility, as is indicated by his intimacy with the
Jewish kings of his day. He was a man of learning and
ability, as is seen from what he said and from his grasp
of the national and world situation of his time. He was
an old bachelor because he thought it wrong to marry and
raise up sons and daughters in a land that was doomed to
destruction, as was his own land. He prophesied in Jerusalem through a period mainly of political and religious
decline and decay. His ministry extended from 626 to 586
B.C.

If ever any man was out of step with the people of his
own generation, that man was the prophet Jeremiah. It
was certainly his difficult lot to clash and quarrel with
the world of his day. For this reason he has been aptly

called the "Rebel Prophet." But while he was constantly
in rebellion, that role was never congenial to him. Though
he went bravely about his task for forty long years, he
never ceased to shrink from it. For this reason, without
any originality I have called him the "Reluctant Prophet."

I

This reluctance to play the part of prophet is evident
through Jeremiah's entire ministry. The fact that he
wrote his story after some twenty-five years of service
may have caused him to give an added emphasis to this
unwillingness. But, be that as it may, one cannot read
his story without realizing that from youth to old age
his ministry was a burden from which he never ceased
to shrink.

1. His reluctance comes out first of all in the story of
his call. When it came home to him as a young man that
God had called him to be a prophet, there was no eagerness in his response. Isaiah was a volunteer. When he
heard the voice of the Lord saying, "Whom shall I send,
and who will go for us?" he made this ready response:
"Here am I; send me." Thus with a spring in his step
and a sparkle in his eye, he set out on his mission. He
seemed eager for the task to which he had been divinely
called.

But such was not the case with Jeremiah. No eager response comes from his lips. He rather asks to be excused.
He begs to be let off for two reasons. The first of these
is his poor equipment for the role of prophet. "I cannot
speak," he pleads. He feels that he is devoid of the

orator's gift. An incapacity to speak may seem a fatal handicap to the prophet. Moses made the same excuse when he heard God's call. But if a lack of capacity to speak may be a heavy handicap, the same may be the case when the preacher has a fatal fluency that enables him to pour out Niagras of words without any serious effort.

Then Jeremiah asks to be excused on account of his youth. "I am a child," he declares. Of course, this was not in reality the case. He was at that time in his middle twenties. To be sure, youth had not then come into its own as it has today. But such youthfulness need not be a handicap to prophecy in any age. The young prophet may find his youthfulness an asset, especially in preaching to his elders. Now and then some church officials will say: "We must have a young preacher in our pulpit so as to appeal to the young people." But a young man makes no special appeal to young people. Generally speaking, his greatest appeal is to old people. Youth is indifferent as to the age of its speaker. Our youngsters are concerned only that the preacher be able to speak their language. Thus Jeremiah showed his unwillingness by his excuse.

This reluctance of the prophet is further seen in God's stern warning. When Jeremiah seeks to excuse himself, God warns him against yielding to his fears. "Be not afraid," he urges, "lest I make you afraid." How is God to frighten his prophet? Not of set purpose, but by natural law. As we defy our fears, they grow weaker and our courage grows stronger. But as we yield to our fears, they grow stronger and our courage grows weaker. If we persistently yield, these fears will become bullies and tyrants. I am thinking of one now who as a boy was somewhat afraid of storms. But through the years he has catered to his fears. He has talked them up until today they are a veritable obsession. Wisely, therefore, does God warn Jeremiah of the peril of yielding to his fears. The need of this warning indicates the prophet's unwillingness to do the task to which he had been called.

Then this reluctance of the prophet is further emphasized, not only by his excuses and God's warning, but by God's encouragements. He virtually says to this shrinking young man: "You are afraid of the difficult task to which I have called you because you feel so unfit. Remember that it is not what you are, but what I am, that counts." You remember the story of that great violinist who came before his audience to find that a cheap fiddle had been substituted for his priceless violin. At first the artist was dismayed. Then he said: "I will show them that the music is not in the violin, but in me."

Even so God encourages Jeremiah by telling him that he will be his sufficiency. He will make him as a fortified city. He will be his strength. Not only so, but he touches his lips saying, "I have put my words in thy mouth." When the minister's lips are divinely touched, he has an eloquence that man cannot permanently gainsay nor resist. There were hundreds of ministers through Moody's generation who had gifts to which this great evangelist was a stranger. Yet in spite of his limitations he gripped his day for God beyond any of them because God had fortified him and had touched his lips with his own divine power. Thus encouraged by God himself, this unwilling prophet began his ministry.

2. Now the reluctance that marked Jeremiah's entrance upon his ministry marked also his entire course. He never seems at any time to have gone with joyous eagerness about his work. In our text he is conducting an imaginary conversation with his mother in which he says:

> "Alas, my mother! you have borne me
> to clash and quarrel with all the world!"

Again in words that we find positively shocking he complains that he was ever born. With bitterness he curses his birthday after the manner of Job. In fact it is probable that the author of the book of Job got his idea for the words of his suffering hero from the reluctant and tortured prophet.

Again we find him making up his mind to quit preaching. He will look upon the abuses and the sins that are ruining his nation and keep silent. Why should he speak? Nobody takes his words to heart. Nobody repents. All the response that people make is to get angry and rebel yet more and more. All that the prophet seems to attain by his faithful preaching is more suffering and more heartache. Naturally, therefore, he resolves to keep silent. But this he cannot do for long, because the word of God is a fire shut in his bones. His strong convictions force him to speak.

Finally, the preacher thinks wistfully of changing his pastorate. He will move. Nowhere is Jeremiah more human than here. He thinks longingly of a lodging place in the wilderness. He wishes for some quiet pastorate among congenial souls where life will not be a persistent battle. With a certain psalmist he is saying, "Oh that I had wings like a dove! for then would I fly away, and be at rest." How many have felt like that! If all in pulpit and pew who have sometimes longed to throw down the whole business and quit were to say amen at once, that amen would doubtless fairly shake the world. The prophet's reluctance comes out, then, in the story of his call. It comes out also in his wail against his lot, in his resolution to be silent, and in his longing to get away.

II

Why was the prophet so reluctant? As we read his story, I think we can detect at least four solid reasons:

1. Jeremiah's reluctance was born in part of his timidity. He was by nature a timid man with quite a modest estimate of his own gifts. He had a natural shrinking from the limelight. To appear before a great and unsympathetic crowd, I am sure, made his knees grow weak with terror. There are some who do not know what timidity means. But perhaps there are yet more who do. As for me, I know how to sympathize with this prophet. I know what it is to have my knees become unmanageable, even in the presence of a congregation that is sympathetic. Such timidity is often quite painful, but it may serve a good purpose. It is likely to save its possessor in some measure from presumptious sin. The timid man is far more likely to make careful preparation than the man who is overconfident.

Blessed is the man whose timidity drives him both to study and to pray.

2. Jeremiah found the role of prophet unwelcome because his message had to be so often a message of denunciation. Of course, it was not purely so. Had such been the case, it would have had little value. It was his business to build and to plant as well as to pluck up and to tear down. But living in an evil day when his nation was headed toward disaster, he could not cry, "Peace, peace," when there was no peace. Instead he had to rebuke again and again. This was very trying on him because he was a sensitive soul deeply in love with both the people and the institutions that he felt called upon to denounce.

All cannot sympathize with the prophet here. There are some ministers who seem to revel in denunciation. There are those who love the clash in battle. I am thinking of one such now. In certain situations he is a genuinely useful man. He was, I think, wisely recommended recently to serve a difficult congregation. In my opinion a man of tough fiber is needed there. As another suggested: "They need a pastor who is a cross between a billy goat and a mule so he can butt at one end and kick at the other." But while the battling prophet sometimes has his place, if his ministry is to be abidingly useful, he must be a great lover. Such was Jeremiah. He suffered in his rebukes far more than those whom he rebuked.

But his own sufferings did not prevent his speaking what he felt to be the truth. Because he loved his people so deeply, he rebuked them with angry eloquence again and again. When, for instance, Jerusalem felt endangered, the wealthy slaveowners within the city resolved to free their Hebrew slaves. They knew that in holding these slaves they were guilty before God and men. Yet when a few days later the danger seemed to lessen, their deathbed repentance was utterly forgotten and they hastened to put their fellow countrymen into slavery again. Against such wickedness the prophet spoke with scathing bitterness.

Jeremiah was deeply religious. He was devoted to the temple as a place of worship. But he recognized the fact that many were making an idol out of the temple. When men first made idols, they did not mean to worship them. They made them as helps to the worship of an unseen God. But by and by they came to fix their eyes upon the means rather than the end. So had these Jews done with regard to the temple. They had come to look to it for protection, to think that because it stood in their sacred city, they were safe in spite of their rebellion against God. Jeremiah, therefore, had to tell them that their faith was futile, that God was going to destroy their temple as he had destroyed the temple at Shiloh.

Jeremiah was an ardent patriot. Yet again and again he had to speak in such fashion as to seem unpatriotic. In fact, he often seemed to his own people little better than a traitor. Desiring to honor his king and to be loyal to him, he had at times to rebuke him to his face. Of one ruler he had to declare that he should be buried with the burial of an ass. When his city was besieged, he did not urge his people to fight to the death, but he rather urged them to surrender. Thus, though deeply loving his people, his church, and his nation, he had to denounce them all and to pronounce their doom. This caused him bitter pain.

3. Then Jeremiah shrank from the prophet's role because of the persecution that his preaching made inevitable. Any man who rebels against his day gets into trouble. We naturally resent folks who are different. This is the secret of the abiding clash between youth and age. Age tends to resent youth, not because youth is necessarily worse than age. The chances are that it will be better. Age resents youth simply because it is different. Likewise youth resents age for the same reason. Of course, the resentment of us who are older is less excusable than theirs. Young people find resentment easy because they have never been old; we often find resentment easy because we have forgotten that we were ever young.

The fact that to be out of step brings persecution is evident wherever we turn. Look at Calvary. Here three men are dying on three separate crosses. Two of them are revolutionaries. They set out in the beginning to strike a blow for freedom. But being unable to organize armies and fight in the open, they became highwaymen. Therefore, they are now paying the penalty for getting too far behind the procession. They are different in that they are somewhat worse than their fellows. But how about this Man who is dying on the central cross? He is being crucified because he got too far ahead of the procession. Society is often a combination to disindividualize the individual and make all of us, as far as possible, as much alike as black-eyed peas. To be too different one way or another is to invite some kind of persecution.

Now persecution was a part of Jeremiah's daily experience. At times he was a laughingstock, at other times he was scorned. One day his neighbors undertook to stone him to death. He had also to know the pain and shame of being put in the stocks. Again he was cast into an old well where there was no water, but where there was mud that gripped him like cold and cruel hands. Here he would have died but for a certain Negro slave who gained the king's permission to set him free. Then when the book that he had written out of the travail of his soul was read by the king, His Majesty in scorn and contempt cut it into bits with his penknife and burned it up. Jeremiah shrank from his task because he hated to denounce the people and institutions that he loved and because he dreaded the persecution that resulted from his denunciation.

4. Finally, the prophet shrank from his task because it seemed so futile, so utterly useless. It is fairly easy to carry on when we are winning. It does not take so much grit to keep climbing if we are getting further up the hill and the air is becoming purer and the outlook more enchanting. But to toil and toil and toil and get nowhere is an experience that is bitter with heartache. Jeremiah had that trying experience beyond any other prophet in the Old Testament. From the beginning to the end he was a lonely voice crying in the wilderness with nobody seemingly paying the least attention to what he said save to answer him with bitter resentment and deeper rebellion. No wonder he shrank

from a ministry that seemed to result in no good to others and only harm to himself.

III

What did this shrinking prophet do with his reluctance?

1. He did not yield to it. Instead he defied it. Though longing to run away, he stood at his post. Though eager to take the easier way of silence, he bravely proclaimed his convictions. Though desperately afraid, he defied his fears and went as bravely upon his appointed course as if he and fear had never met. That is courage of the highest type.

2. Not only did he defy his reluctance, but he used it. He was richer for time and eternity for his reluctance, because he allowed it to drive him closer to God. A strong brave man may confess his need of God, but timid and sensitive souls like Jeremiah must have him. Thus the friendship that he missed among men he found in God. He is constantly speaking to his Lord, sometimes in tender fashion, sometimes in a fashion that sounds to us presumptuous, if not blasphemous. Yet it is doubtful if another man among the prophets was as intimate with God as was Jeremiah.

Living thus in the divine fellowship, this prophet came more and more to be like God. He came to share God's dauntless hopefulness. There are those who think of Jeremiah as a weeping prophet. They think of him as an incorrigible pessimist. But while he wept, he did not weep as those who have no hope. He saw clearly the doom of his own generation. Yet this was only a lost battle, not a lost war. The God of Hope so filled him with joy and peace in believing that he abounded in hope. In spite of his pessimism, he is still one of the most daring optimists among the prophets. While he foresaw the doom of his own generation, while he was sure that his people were going to be driven into exile, he was, I think, the first of the prophets to realize that this exile was to end not in utter loss, but in vast gain. He saw that as a result of this exile his people under God were to learn their richest lessons and to give to the world their finest contribution.

Then with eyes made clear by long fellowship with God, he came also to foresee a better religion than that possessed by the people of his day. Theirs was largely a religion of rules. It was a religion which had to do supremely with the outside of life. This clear-eyed man saw something of the truth which Jesus spoke one night to a master in Israel. He saw that man through coming to know God personally, might be reborn. He believed that one day for every man old things might pass away and all things become new. He learned to sing even in that far-off time:

> "Thy nature, gracious Lord, impart;
>   Come quickly from above,
> Write thy new name upon my heart,
>   Thy new, best, Name of Love."

Here then is a great, tender, and sensitive soul who found the role of prophet very difficult. Seeing with his clear vision, he had to clash and quarrel with the whole world. He found this experience hard because it brought persecution and because his ministry, so far as he could see, was utterly fruitless. But though he was not permitted while in this world to see the results of his faithfulness, yet I am sure that in the land to which he has gone he has seen of the travail of his soul and is satisfied. For while Jeremiah won very meager results in his own lifetime, few, if any, have been so abidingly useful. Therefore we sit at his feet this day, thanking God for a man who so defied and used his fears as to enrich the whole world.

XII

THE MASTER WORKMAN—JEREMIAH

"As the clay is in the potter's hand, so are ye in mine hand."

JEREMIAH 18:6

JEREMIAH WAS CALLED TO GO DOWN TO THE HOUSE OF the potter in order to receive a message from the Lord. As the prophet entered this ancient manufacturing establishment, three objects at once caught and held his attention. First, there was a man at work, the potter. Second, there was that upon which he worked, a bit of clay that was being fashioned into a cup. Third, there was that with which he worked, a wheel. Now this potter with his wheel and his cup has somehow worked his way into the great literature of the world. Clear-eyed men of different centuries have looked at him and have been unable to dismiss him. The great prophet of the exile known as Second Isaiah also saw the potter and was brought under his spell. So, likewise, was Paul of the first century and Omar Khayyám, the Persian poet of the eleventh century. The same is true of Robert Browning, a prophet of the nineteenth century. All these saw the potter and could not forget him.

Naturally these men of genius each saw the potter with his own eyes. Their interpretation of him was conditioned by their faith. Omar Khayyám, for instance, was a fatalist. He had no sense of God. He, therefore, did not see what the men of faith saw. This Persian poet wrote under a gloomy sky. He wrote amidst the fumes of a tavern with a hand that was a bit shaky from too much wine. To him the potter was Fate—blind, heartless, stupid Fate. The cup was man, a creature without a will, deserving, therefore, no more praise for being beautiful than blame for being ugly.

> "They laugh at me for leaning all awry.
>   What! did the hand of the Potter shake?
>
> .   .   .   .
>
>   Some there are who tell
> Of one who threatens he will toss to Hell
>   The luckless Pots he marr'd in making—Pish!
> He's a Good Fellow, and 'twill all be well."

But these prophets of faith had a different reading of things. For them the potter was not blind, stupid Fate, but God, infinite in wisdom and love. The cup was man. The wheel was all the circumstances, the influences, the providences by which God seeks to make man and to bring him to his best. As Browning puts it:

> "He fixed thee 'mid this dance
>   Of plastic circumstance,
>
>   .   .   .   .   .   .

To give thy soul its bent,
Try thee and turn thee forth, sufficiently impressed."

I

Let us look then first at the potter.

1. As Jeremiah entered this ancient manufacturing establishment, he saw a man at work. That man was giving himself to the doing of a certain definite task. He was a specialist, and all his energies were taken up with his work. The potter was a toiler. The same is true of God. Our Lord puts it in this fashion: "My Father worketh even until now, and I work." From eternity to eternity our God is a ceaseless worker. If we are to be kinsfolk with God, we too must work. There is no place in God's plan for an idler.

2. Not only was this potter working, but he was working constructively. He was seeking to make something. This is also true of the Divine Potter. God's primary purpose is always to build. Jesus constantly disclaimed the role of an iconoclast. "Think not that I am come to destroy the law, or the prophets," he affirms. Once when the misguided inhabitants of a certain Samaritan village refused him and his disciples a night's lodging, James and John, sons of thunder that they were, became hot and angry. In their indignation they suggested that they call down fire from heaven and burn them up. But Jesus turned to them with pained amazement looking out from his deep eyes and said: "Ye know not what manner of spirit ye are of. For the Son of man is not come to destroy men's lives, but to save them." God is ever working constructively.

If we are to be laborers together with him, we also must

work constructively. Generally speaking, nothing requires less of heart and less of brains than merely to destroy. A monkey with a match can destroy more in an hour than a thousand men can build in a year. As a young minister I had considerable faith in denunciation. I thought that what many folks needed was a good skinning. But I have discovered that for every one who needs a good skinning there are hundreds who need a good court plaster. It is little good even to destroy evil unless we put good in its place. Even though we might destroy all the tares in our field, if we destroyed the wheat at the same time, we should have only a barren waste.

No wonder, therefore, that this sane old book constantly puts the emphasis on working constructively. "Let everything," said Paul, "be done with a view to building." We are to seek to build up each other. Every attitude that we take, every task that we do, every word that we speak, should be brought to this high test: Will it help to build? To build is costly. It requires work. We can help to destroy an individual, a home, a church, a nation, a world by simply doing nothing at all. God is working constructively. Thus we must work if we are to be laborers together with him.

3. Not only was this potter working constructively; he was working intelligently—that is, according to plan. Had I questioned this potter as to what he proposed to make, would he have had a sensible answer, or would he have said to me: "Don't be silly! You think that with all the vessels I make I have a plan for each one? Certainly not. I simply take a piece of clay, put it upon the wheel, and

trust to luck. If it becomes a vessel of beauty and usefulness, well and good. But if it becomes an ugly, useless
monstrosity, that is all right too. I simply toss it aside. But
I work always at haphazard and never according to plan"?

No sane potter would give that kind of answer or be
guilty of that sort of practice. On the contrary, had I
asked him concerning his purpose for the bit of clay he
had in hand, he would have given a different answer.
"That is just a handful of ugliness you are placing on your
wheel," I might have said. "Yes indeed," he would have
answered, "but it will not always be like that. There is a
place even now where from sordid clay it has become art.
That is in my own mind. I have dreamed a lovely dream
for this piece of clay. Therefore, in spite of its ugliness,
it is on the way to becoming a thing of beauty and usefulness."

Now if this potter who works with clay works according
to plans, surely we may expect no less of God. If this potter
plans every vessel that he makes, even so the Divine Potter
plans every human life. This the Bible teaches over and
over again. Jesus declares that he gives to every man his
work. He affirms that our lives are planned by God as truly
as was his own life. "As thou hast sent me into the world,
even so have I also sent them into the world." Our God
is working according to plan. This he is doing in the life
of the individual. This he is doing also for the nation and
for the world.

Just what is this Divine Potter trying to make of you
and of me? This much we know from his own nature: He
is trying to make us to be beautiful and not ugly. He is

trying to make us helpful and not hurtful. He is trying to make us into creatures like himself. God's purpose for every one of us is that we share the divine nature, that we become more and more like our Lord. He is seeking to make us like him who was glad to lay down his life for others. God sees in every one of us the possibility of Christ-likeness, and he is seeking to bring us to the realization of that fine possibility.

4. As the prophet watched this potter, he discovered that in spite of all his skill he was working with mingled success and failure. He watched him take a bit of clay and transform it rapidly into a vessel of beauty. Then he saw him take a second piece that looked just as promising and seemed to have just as many possibilities; but, as he was changing that from ugliness to beauty, something went wrong. "The vessel that he made of clay was marred in the hand of the potter." Though he had dreamed as lovely a dream for the clay that went into this marred vessel as for that which went into the vessel of beauty, he did not realize that dream.

Now as this ancient potter worked with mingled success and failure, even so does the Divine Potter. That sounds a bit shocking I know. Is not our God an Almighty God? Is there no truth in that glad shout "the Lord God Omnipotent reigneth"? There is. But the fact that God is King does not mean that he is a despot. He will force no man to conform to his will. Therefore, he cannot always make you and me what he longs for us to be. He cannot make of the nations what he longs to make. Certainly he has not planned that this world with its rich possibilities should be the torn and tortured thing that it is today. Of course, we are not to conclude that failure in the present means that failure is to be final. All we are affirming is that God, the infinite worker, is now working with mingled success and failure.

II

Why this failure? Why, as we look abroad today, does it seem

> "As if some lesser god had made the world,
> But had not force to shape it as he would?"

Why is it that with an infinite God as our Father, we are often such spiritual failures? Why is our poverty so glaring when we set it down beside the vast wealth that is offered to us over and over again throughout the pages of his Book? Why are we human cups so often marred in the making? Not one of us has achieved the fullness of his possibilities. Why is this the case?

Glance for a moment at this ancient potter. Why did he fail? It was not because he had no skill. He was a specialist. It was not because he was indifferent to his work. He was seeking earnestly to do his task well. It was because there was something in the clay that resisted him. He failed because there was some bit of stubborness in the clay that made the realization of his purpose impossible. He simply could not make of the material in hand the vessel that he longed to make.

Why then, I repeat, does God fail? It is not because of

any lack of wisdom on his part. He knows what you and I are capable of becoming. It is not because he is not doing his very best for us. This, I know, some find hard to believe. There are many who are convinced that God could do far more for them than he is doing if he were not too narrow-minded in judging their innocent little sins, and just a bit niggardly with his blessings. But God is doing his sacrificial best for every human soul. There is no price that he is not willing to pay in order to realize his purpose in and through us. The Cross is a proof of that. The plain truth is that God is doing everything for us that we will permit him to do. But just as this clay resisted the potter, so we resist God. Of course, there is this difference between us and the clay: the clay has no will, no power of choice. We have. We can say yes to God or we can say no to him. God, I repeat, never coerces. He never encroaches upon our freedom. He has too great a respect for human personality for that. All he will ever do is to stand at the door and knock. Therefore, the weakest of us may thwart his purpose in our lives if we so desire. All that is wrong in us, all that is wrong in our broken world, has its source here: We have refused to do the will of God.

III

What did the potter do with this vessel that was marred in his hand?

I know what I should have expected him to do. I should have expected him to have taken the whole miserable affair and tossed it aside. Why seek to conserve a piece of clay when there was plenty more where that came from? But instead of tossing the clay aside he started all over again making another vessel as seemed good to the potter to make it.

This, too, is the way of the Divine Potter. When we go wrong, when we resist him, when we make a mess of life by defying his will, he does not give us up. He does not throw us away. With a persistent patience beyond all belief he seeks to make us again. This is called the gospel of the second chance. It is far more. It is the gospel of all but endless chances. The God that calls on us to forgive until seventy times seven will surely do no less himself.

But suppose this potter that the prophet watched had failed a second time and a third and a fourth. He might have still persisted. Yet in the nature of things he could not go on endlessly. This is the case because the clay is becoming less and less plastic. By and by it will become so hard that the skilled fingers of the potter can no longer mold it into shape. If you step outside the potter's house, you will find yourself in the potter's field. At once you will hear the crunching of broken crockery under your feet. Why is this broken earthenware here? Does the potter make vessels for the purpose of breaking them? By no means. These broken pieces of clay are the fragments of vessels that might have been, had the clay not resisted the potter.

Is it possible for us to defeat the purposes of the Divine Potter? So far as we can see in the here and now, we must anwer in the affirmative. This is true both of individuals and of nations. God could not realize his purpose in the great nations of the ancient world. Flinging themselves outside the will of God, they smashed themselves against God's judgments. God could not realize his purposes even for Israel. There is the very heartache of God in that sob of the Master: "O Jerusalem, Jerusalem, which killest the prophets, and stonest them that are sent unto thee; how often would I have gathered thy children together, as a hen doth gather her brood under her wings, and ye would not!" (Luke 13:34.) What was the outcome? The city was destroyed in one of the most horribly bloody sieges that our world has ever known.

We heve emerged from the most tragic war in all history. We won the victory. How shall we look upon this victory? We can look upon it, as another suggests, in one of three ways.

First, we can affirm that we won simply because we were stronger than our foes. We had more men and more equipment; therefore we defeated them and brought them to their knees. But if that is all we see, our victory is only a jumble of bloody nonsense

Second, we can say that we won because we were right and our enemies were wrong. We were on God's side, and they were on the side of the devil. They had nothing to say for themselves. We had everything to say for ourselves. But to take this position would be a bit of ghastly pharisaism that would, if possible, be more runious than defeat.

A third position that we can take is that in spite of our sins God brought us through to give us and our bleeding world another chance. God in his infinite love and patience is now setting himself to remake the world that we have wrecked. He has to make that world through human hands.

May we not believe that we ourselves have come to the kingdom for such a time as this? But believe me, God can use us just in proportion as we are loyal to his will. Except the Lord build this great world-house, they labor in vain that build it.

What can you and I as mere individuals do about it? Well, we can do this. We can each furnish one life so fully dedicated to God, so filled with his Spirit that our homes, our church, our nation, and our world will be the stronger by our having lived. Give yourself to God, then, and he will accept you. Give him yourself, and he will remake you. Give him yourself, and he will use you and enable you increasingly to know through your own experience "what is that good, and acceptable, and perfect, will of God."

> Have thine own way, Lord!
>   Have thine own way!
> Thou art the Potter;
>   I am the clay.
> Mold me and make me
>   After thy will,
> While I am waiting
>   Yielded and still.
>
> Have thine own way, Lord!
>   Have thine own way!
> Hold o'er my being
>   Absolute sway!
> Fill with thy spirit
>   Till all shall see
> Christ only, always,
>   Living in me! [1]

[1] Adelaide A. Pollard, "Have Thine Own Way, Lord." Copyrighted by Hope Publishing Company.

XIII

MARKED MEN—EZEKIEL

"But come not near any man upon whom is the mark."

EZEKIEL 9:6

THIS IS A PART OF ONE OF THE MOST STRIKING AND AR-resting of the visions of the prophet Ezekiel. In this vision God called unto himself a man who had a writer's inkhorn by his side. He then sent this man through the streets of Jerusalem, commanding him to set a mark upon the foreheads of the men who sighed and cried for all the abominations that were done in the midst of the city. This done, God commanded others to follow the man with the inkhorn and to slay without mercy everyone whose brow was not marked. Only the marked men were to be spared. It seems, at first sight, a heartless and cruel procedure. Yet, when rightly understood, it is in harmony with the Bible as a whole; it is especially in harmony with the teaching of the New Testament; it is more especially still in harmony with the teaching of Jesus.

I

This scene is a kind of judgment day. God is here making a distinction between one man and another. We have a great tendency to judge men in the mass. We judge them by their nearness to each other, or by the organizations to which they belong. "He is a Protestant," we say, or, "He is a Catholic," or, "He belongs to a labor union." We also judge men by their race. "Oh yes," we say, as if that were explanation enough, "he is a Negro." Again we affirm: "Germans are always Germans," or, "Japanese are always Japanese." Thus we imply that all of one particular race are alike. Nathaniel was a good man, but he came very near to missing Jesus because he judged people in the mass. He made up his mind that, because the Master came from Nazareth, a city of bad reputation, he must not be worth knowing.

But, while we thus judge men in the mass, God always looks to the individual. He never allows the nearness of one to another to confuse him. "I tell you," said Jesus, "in that night there shall be two men in one bed; the one shall be taken, and the other shall be left. Two women shall be grinding together; the one shall be taken, and the other left." These people were so close together physically that they could have touched each other, yet spiritually they were as far apart as the spaces between the stars. However near we are together, God always distinguishes you from me, and me from you. Thus, as God looked upon this ancient city, he saw men as individuals and distinguished one from the other.

Distinguishing man from man, God divided them into two groups. There is nothing unique about this. Jesus constantly divided folks into two groups. As he looked upon the world of his day, he saw some who were traveling by the broad road, while others were traveling by the narrow. There were those who were building on foundations of sand and those who were building on foundations of rock. There were those who were spiritually alive and those who were spiritually dead. There were those who were ready for life's emergencies and those who were not ready. The prophet Ezekiel here divided men into two groups—those who care and those who do not care—those who sigh and cry for all the abominations that were being done in the midst of the city and those who are indifferent.

Now this charge of indifference is about the worst possible. One of the ugliest episodes in all the Bible takes place in the temple. Judas has betrayed his Lord. For this he is now sorry to the point of utter desperation. The thirty pieces of silver that he has won by his treachery feel hot as live coals in his bosom. What does he do? Where does he turn when his blackest hour is upon him? Being a religious man, he hurries to his church—to the temple. He turns to the priests, whose business it is to help him. In their presence he flings down the money and sobs: "I have sinned in that I have betrayed the innocent blood." Then what? Do these men weep with him? Do they seek in any way to help him? By no means. They merely shrug their shoulders and answer: "What is that to us? see thou to that." They do not lay the weight of their hands upon Judas, yet their treatment of him is, literally, as cruel as hell.

But this other group—the people upon whose foreheads the man with the inkhorn had set his mark—what of them? They were people who cared, people who simply could not let well enough alone. Of course, the fact that these sighed and cried means far more than that they merely shed a few maudlin tears. Tears can be very cheap. I have known a few people who could turn them on as easily as we turn on the faucet in the bathroom. There are those who fancy that they are very tenderhearted merely because they can weep. Having wept, they go their way feeling they have done their full duty. I once knew of a boat whose engine was so weak that every time it whistled it had to stop and get up steam again. This whistle was akin to the tears of those who are satisfied with mere weeping. But the tears of those that sighed and cried indicated that they cared so deeply that, to the extent of their ability, they were willing to help.

Years ago J. Wilbur Chapman asked Sam Hadley to show him over some of the slums about his Water Street mission. For several hours they went together through those haunts of shame and suffering. Then Dr. Chapman, feeling that he had seen all he could bear, told his companion good night and started back to his hotel. He had gone only a few steps when he heard a groan. Looking back, he saw Hadley with his face in his hands. Fearing that he had been taken suddenly ill, he hurried back to ask what was wrong. Then Hadley, as he turned his pain-pinched face toward the scenes they had just visited, said: "Oh, the sin, the suffering of those people! It will break my heart. It has broken my heart." Because it broke his heart, he fished out of the slums hundreds of those desperate souls who came to walk as victors where they had before gone down in defeat.

147

Let us look then at these two groups.

II

First, the indifferent. There were certain people in that distant day who managed to live in a city that was threatening to rot down morally and yet remain indifferent to its danger. When good men were so desperately needed to stand in the gap, to serve as saving salt, it was simply none of their business. Confronted by political and moral disaster that they might have helped to avert, they somehow managed to be concerned only for themselves. There were no marks of care for others on their faces. They never lost an hour's sleep over the tragic plight of their toppling nation. They passed through the whole trying experience without receiving one single wound while fighting for others. What came of it? What did their indifference do for them?

Well, for one thing, it saved them a lot of expense and work. When an offering was taken, those soliciting soon learned to pass them by. When time and effort were needed, they always had business of their own to look after. Though for cenutries men have condemned the priest and Levite who passed that wounded man on the highway, yet these have this to say for themselves: They got home in time for dinner. Not only so, but they got home without any bloodstains either upon their hands or upon their garments. They reached home also with all the oil, wine, and bandages with which they set out. Thus those who cannot be bothered by the needs of others do save themselves considerable expense both in money and in time and effort.

At last they may be able to slip out of life a bit like the gentleman of whom Charles Lamb writes: "He passed away, dying as he lived, without much trouble."

But if by refusing to care these saved themselves a lot of trouble, they also missed a great deal which they surely would have liked. Caring only for themselves, they missed the joy of usefulness. They missed the thrill of having the hand of some grateful man grip theirs with an appreciation that could not be put into words. "I will bless thee," said God to Abraham, "and thou shalt be a blessing." To receive a blessing is a great privilege, but to be a blessing is the very poetry of living. These people missed that poetry because they did not care.

Not only did these with unmarked brows miss the joy of being a blessing, but to a man they were put to the sword. That sounds harsh I know. But this is the prophet's dramatic way of saying what Jesus said centuries later and what experience confirms: "Whosoever shall seek to save his life shall lose it." To live for self alone, to stand from under the needs and burdens of others is simply to refuse to have any life at all that is worthy of the name. This truth Jesus enforced over and over again.

For instance, our Lord told the story of a highly successful farmer who made such a bumper crop that he had to tear down his old barns and build greater in order to take care of his rich harvest. When we look in upon this man, he is very busy at barn building. Even so, he is not concerned with material things alone. Busy as he is with his building program, he still has a little time to give to his soul. We see him as he administers this bit of artificial respiration: "Soul, thou hast much goods laid by for many years; . . . eat, drink, and be merry." "It is true," he seems to say, "that you do not have anything to live for, but you have such a lot to live on. So cheer up!"

What is the matter with this farmer? How is it that, while some of him has lived, the most of him has died? We can learn the answer by listening to him think. We cannot always tell what a man is by looking at him. "There's no art to find the mind's construction in the face." We cannot always tell what he is by hearing him talk. He may speak truth with his lips to which his heart is a stranger. But when we hear him think, we know him for what he is. "As a man thinketh in his heart, so is he." Listen then to his thinking. "He thought within himself, saying, What shall I do because I have no room where to bestow my fruits? And he said, This will I do: I will pull down my barns, and build greater; and there will I bestow all my fruits and my goods."

Here then the man reveals himself. Of what does he think? He thinks of himself, of his crops, of his barns, of his own soul. That in itself is not bad. But the tragedy lies in what he forgets. He is so busy thinking about himself that he forgets God and he forgets his brother. It does seem that he might have thought of how good God had been to him in sending him sunshine and rain at just the right time and in just the right proportion. It seems also that he might have thought of those who had worked for him and with him and made his success possible. It surely seems that he might have thought of those whose barns were not only not overflowing but almost empty. But, thinking only of himself, he shows himself a fool and dies at last without ever having known the joy of real living.

When that graceless laddie left home in another of the stories of Jesus, his going cast a black shadow over his father's life. But it would seem that this father still had much for which to be thankful. His elder son did not follow the steps of the prodigal. On the contrary, he remained at home and worked. He was also very obedient. He reminded his father a little later that he had never broken a single one of his commandments, and this his father did not deny. But in spite of his energy and obedience, this elder son brought his sorrowing father little joy.

Why was this the case? For one reason, when his father kept going to that vantage point that gave him the farthest view toward the far country, he always had to go alone. His elder son never went with him. Then one day, when he saw the prodidgal a great way off and ran to fall on his neck and kiss him, he was still alone—the elder son was not there. When the great feast was prepared, again the elder son was not present. Why? It was not because he was not wanted. His father went out and begged him to come in. He was not present because he could not be. God himself cannot give the feast of life to one who is self-centered. Therefore, while these unmarked souls dodged a good many difficulties, they missed the joy of usefulness, they missed the joy of everything that is worthy of the name of life.

> "She built herself a little house
> All walled around with pride,

Took Prudence for her servant
And shut herself inside.

"She drew her blinds down tight as tight
When sorrow chanced to roam.
Experience called, she sent down word
That she was not at home.

"Then wherefore should she now complain,
And wherefore should she sigh,
If life and love and laughter
Have passed unseeing by?"

III

But how about the marked men? Those that sigh and cry?

1. They had to do a lot of work and a lot of giving. Not only so, but they had to undergo a lot of suffering which they might have escaped. Carlyle tells of a certain insect in the South Sea Islands which when wounded gives off in its agony a kind of light. The natives sometimes thrust these insects through with a spear and hold them above their heads to light their way through the jungles. Good for the natives, but what about the insects? Of course, it was helpful to this ancient city to have a few people who took its needs seriously, but how about the people themselves? Well, finding it impossible to let the burdens of others alone, they had, I repeat, both to suffer and to give.

Jesus was such a man. I can imagine sitting down by a citizen of Nazareth a few years after Calvary and asking about that young carpenter. "Yes," he might have said, "he used to own that little shop down the street. He was a first class carpenter, too. Was getting along very well, and might have made a good living; but one day he shut up shop to go about doing good, as one of his followers put it. But instead of making friends of folks who could help his cause, he gathered about him a few nameless souls, none of whom helped him, while some did him nothing but harm. No wonder he ended on a cross."

But we are not to let the fact that Jesus lived in the spirit of the cross and died at last on that skull-shaped hill blind us to the truth that he lived richly, abundantly, joyously. In spite of the fact that he suffered in the suffering of others to a superlative degree—yes, and because of that fact—his was the most radiant life ever lived in this world. He declared that the yoke which he wore was kindly. So abundantly did he live that the people of his day were constantly asking him how they might lay hold of life. He was so joyous that many of the woefully religious thought him little better than one of the wicked.

To what did he owe this joy? Certainly not to the fact that he settled down comfortably and let his brother's burden alone. He lived thus richly because he cared so deeply that he lived a life of complete self-giving. It was out of his own experience that he spoke that strange word, "Blessed are they that mourn." It sounds like a contradiction, as if he were saying, "Joyful are the joyless. Happy are the unhappy." Yet what he says is literally true. The only really joyful folks are the burdened folks. There is more gladness even in their tears than in the laughter of the self-centered.

Therefore, if these marked men had a good deal of trouble that they might have escaped, they at least lived, and that richly. It is ever so. When we seek for the man of the New Testament who, with the exception of the Master himself, lived most abundantly, we find that man in Paul. But what a stormy and hard life he lived! Sometimes we find him at the whipping post. Again he is clinging to a bit of wreckage in the sea. Then we see him in a dungeon shivering with cold. Always he is burdened by the care of all the churches. At times he is so broken in heart over the rebellion of his own people that he catches himself wishing that he might be accursed of God for their sakes. Yet we never find him without a song of joyful thanksgiving upon his lips. The more he dies, the more richly he lives. His was the joy of a man who cared.

What then has this to say to you and to me? For some reason God is matching us against one of the most desperate hours of human history. It would seem that our world was never more darkened by tragedy. Some of this tragedy is far away. Some is as near as our own city, our own church, our own neighbors, our own fireside. What is our attitude toward the pressing needs of our day? If the man with the inkhorn were to pass in and out among us today, would he put his mark upon your brow and mine? Remember that if he has to pass us by, all that is worthy of the name of life passes with him. It is the marked men who live, and they only.

XIV

THE POWER OF PREACHING —EZEKIEL

"Prophesy upon these bones, and say unto them, O ye dry bones, hear the word of the Lord. . . . Behold, I will cause breath to enter into you, and ye shall live."

EZEKIEL 37:4-5

I

THIS TEXT HAS AN INTERESTING BACKGROUND. IN 597 B.C. Jerusalem fell to the forces of Babylon. Though the conquerors left the city unharmed—to stand for eleven more years under a puppet king—they immediately carried into exile some ten thousand of her choicest citizens. Among these was a brilliant prophet by the name of Ezekiel. This prophet was destined in the providence of God to become a maker of history. His influence upon his own people was to be very great. He became in a sense the father of Judaism. He spoke with power to the people of his day. He speaks still to those who have ears to hear.

Now in this long and tearful trek from Jerusalem to Babylon, Ezekiel with his fellow captives, in all probability, passed through a wide-stretching valley where a battle had been fought long months before. This had been a great conflict. The slain on both sides were many. When, the battle was over, it would seem that both armies withdrew, leaving their dead unburied. The beasts of the field, the birds of the air, and the forces of nature had had their way with these dead bodies. There was not even a skeleton left whole. There were only shattered bones whitening in the sun. The horrid scene stretched in every direction as far as the eye could see. It was a veritable valley of death. The ghastly ugliness of it left a lasting impression upon Ezekiel's mind.

A few years later he was called to prophesy to his people who were in exile. When he confronted this congregation, so tragic was their plight that they reminded him of the valley of dry bones. These people were living in what amounted to a concentration camp on the banks of the river or canal of Chebar not far from Babylon. They had suffered greatly. They had lost their homes. They had lost their native land. They had lost friends and loved ones. Many had lost their faith in God. They were telling themselves: "Our bones are dry; our hope is lost; we are cut off." Thus they were embittered and desperate, without even a horizon where they might hope for a dawn. But God was ready to make bare his arm. Therefore, they were facing, not toward death, but toward life.

II

How was their recovery brought about?

1. The first move toward recovery was made on the

part of God. This is ever the case. Man's search for God is very impressive. It is the oldest and most persistent of all human quests. When Philip said, "Lord, shew us the Father, and it sufficieth us," he was voicing a longing that is as old as man. It was uttered long before Abraham left Ur of the Chaldees to journey into the unknown. It was uttered ages before the towers of Babylon lifted their tall heads to gaze down on the smiling waters of the Euphrates. It is a quest that is the very mother of religion. No nation has ever been so cultivated or so backward as to be entirely without it.

But if man's quest for God is impressive, God's quest for man is still more impressive. This is the case because it is God's quest for man that explains man's quest for God. We would not seek him unless we had first been sought. "We love him because he first loved us." If you are possessed of a single longing for a better life, if you come into God's house with the least hunger for goodness, with the slightest hatred of evil, that means that you do not come alone. Our very restlessness, our dissatisfaction with life as we are living it, our tormenting fears—all these are but the footfalls of the Good Shepherd out in quest of the sheep that is lost.

2. Not only did God make the first move toward the recovery of these broken people, but the remedy was of his own choosing. How did God go about the realization of his purpose for these people? It is significant that he passed by many remedies that we have found helpful and on which we have come to depend. For instance, he did not set his prophet to organizing these bones, to matching

bone with bone in order to tie them into skeletons. No more did he command the prophet to polish the bones. However highly polished dry bones may be, they will still be dead and incapable of doing anything but disintegrating.

In the realization of this we do not worship at the shrine of education as enthusiastically as our fellows of a few years ago. We have learned that education which is of the head only may be an unmitigated curse. We have learned that science in the hands of men without religious faith may become a supreme killer. Unless we get God into our education, it will serve us no better than the training of Prospero served Caliban in Shakespeare's *Tempest*. "Thou hast taught me speech," declared the monster in all bitterness, "and the profit of it is that I can curse." We have been so taught that we can help and heal. We can also destroy beyond the dreams of a bloody yesterday.

No more did God command his prophet to prepare a purely social program. He did not send him to guarantee for every man a job with adequate wages and a comfortable house in which to live. Not that these things are unimportant. They are vastly important. But they are not first. They are not the abundant life of which Jesus speaks. It is possible for people to have all these things and yet be tortured by their own spiritual poverty. It is quite possible for a community to be well clothed, well fed, well housed, well educated, and well rotted all at the same time.

What then, I repeat, was God's remedy? The answer sounds so futile and foolish that the man of the world is tempted to laugh out loud at the very mention of it. It seems so impotent as to be little short of madness. God told his prophet that the way out for these broken and hopeless people was to hear the word of the Lord. He commanded his prophet to preach to this audience of dry bones.

III

Now it strikes me that God's confidence in preaching ought to renew our confidence in that important work. Through the years it has pleased God by the foolishness of preaching to save them that believe. Throughout the Bible preaching and salvation are related to each other as cause and effect. "Whosoever shall call upon the name of the Lord shall be saved. How then shall they call upon him in whom they have not believed? and how shall they believe in him of whom they have not heard? and how shall they hear without a preacher?" A writer in a certain magazine said some time ago that the least farmer in the United States contributed more to human well-being than the best minister. Well, about this I will not argue further than to say that he and God do not see things alike. God has always set great store by preaching.

We need to bear this in mind today in order to recover our faith in the work of preaching. Of course, preaching is not the task of the pulpit alone, but also of the pew. All of us preach. We preach in our homes. We preach to our friends. We preach in our places of business. Sometimes we preach consciously—always we preach unconsciously—by the lives we live. But I feel there is a special word that I ought to say in behalf of the man that is called to prophesy in the pulpit. This is the case because so much is being done to keep the modern minister from what I consider to be his supreme task, that of preaching.

1. Often preaching is sidetracked because the work of the modern minister is so many-sided. There is no other man in the community from whom so much is expected. The modern minister must be an organizer and an executive. He must be a financier. He must be wise to the educational program of the church. He must be a pastor. He must be a citizen of his community. He cannot confine his ministry within the four walls of his church or to his own congregation. The early apostles confronted by a multitude of tasks reached this wise decision, "It is not reason that we should leave the word of God, and serve tables. . . . But we will give ourselves continually to prayer, and to the ministry of the word." Not all ministers are thus wise. But we need to bear in mind that no man can preach unless he has time to prepare to preach.

2. The modern minister, with so many calls upon his time, decides sooner or later that he cannot do everything. Having made this decision, he does not always make a choice of the highest task. Often he majors on the task that is most congenial. Since we are all constitutionally lazy, too often the congenial task is not the one that is most important, but the one that is easiest. Hence he neglects his preaching. The man who seeks the easy way will always neglect preaching, because preaching is difficult. In fact, I am convinced that the right kind of preaching is the most costly of all work. It takes great pains and practice, one has suggested, to learn to paint well. How much of hard work goes into the attainment of that skill that enables the

artist so to capture the human face that when you look at the picture you see your father or your mother! But how much more difficult so to capture the face of Jesus and so to picture it in words that those who hear will see him as the fairest of ten thousand and one altogether lovely! We tend therefore to neglect preaching because it is so costly.

3. Then preaching often has to take second place because of the new emphasis that is being placed on worship. Now this new emphasis is all to the good. Nothing can be more important than worship. Yet, believing with all my heart in the goal, I mistrust some of the roads by which we seek to attain that goal. I have witnessed worship programs that would have been laughable had they not been so pathetic. Why we can worship better in the dimness of a smoking, smelly candle than by an electric light has never been explained to me satisfactorily. I know that no less an authority than John Milton speaks of a "dim religious light." Yet surely light is not religious in proportion to its dimness. To assume that such is the case is to forget that God is Light, as the New Testament says, and to believe instead that he is only twilight.

Then I think we make a serious blunder when we draw a line between the so-called worship service and the sermon. When we go to church we go to public worship. Of course we are supposed to worship through our songs and prayers. But if the service has any wholeness about it, we ought also to worship through the sermon. In fact, the sermon ought to bring our worship to its climax. Therefore I cannot agree with those who are displacing the prophet by the priest. In public worship I have been helped many times by the prayers. I have been helped by the great hymns—those stairways of the spirit upon which aspiring souls have through the years climbed up to God. But, speaking out of my own experience, I must confess that I have said with the greatest penitence, "God be merciful to me a sinner," and have felt with deepest awe and gladness, "Surely God is in this place," when some prophet of the Lord, whether of vast ability or mediocre ability, has preached in such a fashion as to compel me to believe that his lips had been freshly touched with a live coal from off heaven's own altar.

This also I must add. Even when I have found the so-called worship service helpful, if the minister has followed with a shoddy, ill-prepared, and slovenly delivered sermon, much of the good gained has been dissipated. Therefore, I am fully convinced that there is nothing more important to a service of public worship than the right kind of preaching. In fact, the kind of church, the kind of community, the kind of nation we are going to have tomorrow, depend largely upon the kind of preaching that is being done in our pulpits and upon the response that we make to that preaching. Preaching, therefore, is not a matter of second importance but of supreme importance. It is highly significant that Jesus, who could have given himself to so many great tasks, gave his little handful of years to preaching.

IV

How may the minister hope to speak effectively? He can learn something from the experience of Ezekiel. What was his equipment?

1. Ezekiel was in touch with God. That is fundamental. "The hand of the Lord was there upon me," he declares. That is to be our equipment, whatever form our preaching may take. It has been the equipment of every man who has spoken effectively. Not even Jesus would undertake his ministry without being thus empowered. In his own home church he took the words of Isaiah upon his lips and made them his very own as he declared, "The Spirit of the Lord is upon me, because he hath anointed me to preach." As we go about the high task of making God known to men, he gives us the assurance of his presence, "Go ye therefore, and make disciples, . . . and, lo, I am with you always, even unto the end of the world."

2. Not only was Ezekiel in touch with God; he was also in touch with men. When God called him to the ministry, before the prophet preached a single sermon, he came to a sympathetic understanding of those to whom he was to preach. "I sat where they sat," he tells us. He put himself in the place of his people. He looked out on life through their eyes. He wept through their tears. He bled through their wounds. He struggled under the weight of their burdens. Thus he came to possess the rare treasure of an understanding heart. God has to have men in the pulpit who know folks—how they are born, how they live, how they

die. Every minister must do some pastoral work, if not for the good of his people, then for the good of his own soul. To lose touch with people is to lose the power to preach. The real preacher must stay in touch both with God and with man.

3. Finally, the preacher must preach simply, so that the humblest person who comes in search of the bread of life will not be disappointed. He must speak positively and constructively. He must speak hopefully. He must speak expectantly, with the firm assurance that God is adequate for the most hopeless situation in the life of the individual or of the community. Thus did Ezekiel speak. This was his positive and heartening word: "Ye shall live." That is my message. Whatever may have been the failings of yesterday, however dead in heart and hope you may be, if you will hear the word of the Lord and give God a chance, you shall live.

V

As the preacher in touch with God and man thus spoke the word of God with conviction, what happened? Did anything happen? Do we expect anything to happen when we come together in our services Sunday by Sunday?

As the prophet preached, the whole hopeless situation was changed. Death gave place to life. The valley of dry bones was transformed into a parade ground for the army of the King. Similar situations have changed when men in the power of God have preached throughout the years. The rushing of the mighty wind at Pentecost, the fiery tongues —these were not the climax of that service. The service

164

reached its climax when a man stood up to preach. It was then that three thousand were added unto the Lord.

Centuries later when the Dark Ages had settled over Europe, how was the night banished and how did the day dawn? It came about through preaching, especially through the preaching of Martin Luther. Later still, when England had become little better spiritually than the valley of dry bones, how did the dead church of that day come to a resurrection? It was through the preaching of John Wesley and his followers. Believe me, the world needs nothing today quite so much as it needs the right kind of preaching.

But why do I say this to you in the pew? Because preaching is a co-operative task. The effectiveness of any sermon depends quite as much upon the pew as upon the pulpit—sometimes, I fancy, even more. How you can help by your presence, your labors, your sympathy, especially your prayers! Many a preacher who seems prosaic and dead would be clothed with new life and power if his own people would really pray for him. This was surely the faith of Paul. He never wrote a single letter, except to the backslidden church of Galatia, without asking for the prayers of his people. He believed that the most nameless nobody, the poorest slave in all the Roman Empire, could by his prayers anoint his apostolic lips with wisdom, grace, and power. In this day of need let us—ministers and people, pulpit and pew—rededicate ourselves to the high, co-operative task of preaching.

XV

ARE YOU SATISFIED?
—SECOND ISAIAH

"Wherefore do ye spend money for that which is not bread, and your labor for that which satisfieth not?"

ISAIAH 55:2

HERE IS A MAN SPEAKING ON BEHALF OF GOD. HE MUST have been a great soul—this we know, though we do not know his name. I think we may be sure that the scholars are right in affirming that this is not the same man who speaks to us in the first half of the great book of Isaiah. Why he is nameless we do not know. It may be that he was so busy doing his work that he failed to leave his autograph. It is more likely that he failed to give us his name because of the nature of his message. It was his mission to comfort his exiled people by assuring them that God would destroy Babylon and thus set them free. In the great passage of which our text is a part he is pointing them to God as their one hope. "Wherefore," he questions, "do ye spend money for that which is not bread, and your labor for that which satisfieth not?"

I

To whom is the prophet speaking?

1. His question is addressed to the dissatisfied of his own day. There were men all about him who were leading starved lives. His question is addressed also to the dissatisfied of every day. Therefore it has something to say to us. Who are the dissatisfied? They are those who for some reason have not arrived. They are the ones who feel that life has not, for them at least, measured up. Satisfaction comes from two Latin words: *satis,* "enough"; and *facio,* "to make." He is speaking to the people who have not yet found enough to meet their needs. That, I take it, is a great company.

You notice that in speaking to these who are not satisfied, the prophet is not assuming that all such are profligates. Naturally, some of those who are dissatisfied may have gone terribly wrong. Some of them have perhaps gone into the far country, where they have wasted their substance with riotous living. Some are having to confess to themselves that, instead of finding satisfaction, they have found starvation. This word is certainly addressed to those who have to say, "I perish with hunger," but it is not for them alone.

If the prophet is speaking to those who have wasted their substance with ritous living, he is speaking no less to others who are quite decent and respectable. His question is addressed to many who are earnestly religious. It is, for instance, addressed to such men as the rich young ruler. In him we see a man who, in spite of the fact that he has been clean from his youth, in spite of the fact that he is courageous and in love with the best, yet has to confess that he is not satisfied. With his face one gaunt wistfulness, he hurries to fling himself at the Master's feet with this question upon his lips, "What lack I yet?" Since, therefore, the prophet is speaking to all who are dissatisfied, his question may be very personal to you and me.

2. The prophet's question is addressed not only to the dissatisfied, but to those who are making pathetic and futile efforts to find satisfaction. Man has never quite been able to worship the god of things as they are. Almost all the silly and stupid things we do, as well as those that are beautiful and wise, grow out of our efforts to find satisfaction. The man who gets drunk is seeking, by getting relief from himself, to find satisfaction. Those who crowd the night spots of the world are not madly seeking to wreck themselves or to hurt others; they are only seeking in this fashion to find satisfaction.

Just as this quest leads to our doing foolish things, it leads also to our doing things that are wise and worth while. There came a day when man was not satisfied with the rude bed on which he was accustomed to sleep, so he made a better bed. He was not satisfied with his rude cave, so he built a shack, then a cottage, a castle, a palace. He was not satisfied with his means of transportation, so be built a wagon, a boat, a train, a car, an airship. He was not satisfied with his means of communication, so he invented language, printing, the telephone, the telegraph, the wireless. In making all these he was seeking to enrich life. He has achieved much, yet it is doubtful whether by all these gadgets he has gained one ounce of real satisfaction.

The men to whom the prophet spoke were all seekers, but, as is the case today, only the few were finders.

3. Finally, the prophet is speaking not only to those who are dissatisfied and who are making futile efforts to find satisfaction, but to those who refuse to learn either from the experience of others or from their own experience. It has been wisely said that experience is a hard teacher but that fools will learn from no other. And a great many fools will not learn even from that. The people of the prophet's day seemed to enjoy being humbugged. The road they took yesterday led them to no worthy goal. Yet they were taking the same road today. They were making the same foolish investments, trading at the same booths, being duped by the same tricksters.

But surely we cannot throw stones at these because of their refusal to learn. By so doing we should only endanger ourselves. We, too, have been slow to learn. For instance, every time we have sought to save our lives, we have lost. Every time we have shrugged our shoulders and declared, "Every fellow for himself, and the devil take the hindmost," we have found the devil getting the foremost as well. Every time we have tried to look out for number one, either individually or nationally, we have been cheated. Yet we are so slow to learn that the prophet looks at each of us, hardly able to believe what he sees, and questions: "Wherefore do ye spend money for that which is not bread, and your labor for that which satisfieth not?"

> "At the devil's booth are all things sold,
>   Each ounce of dross costs its ounce of gold."

Still we refuse to seek another booth.

II

Now what does this prophet have to say to those who are making vain efforts to find satisfaction?

His is a wise and heartening word. He does not tell us that our quest must be futile and that we must be content with whatever dusty nothings we may have been able to win. He knows that, if we have failed to find satisfaction, it is not because no such goal is possible but because we have sought in the wrong direction. He knows too that our failure to find the satisfaction for which we long, while disappointing, is at once the badge of our greatness and the prophecy of our future victory. However far wrong we may go, hell never really begins until we force ourselves to be satisfied with what we are.

When, for instance, Faust sold himself to the devil, he was in a bad way. But even then he was not utterly hopeless. He was given to understand that his case would never be hopeless so long as he was not contented with the bad bargain that he had made. If ever he should find entire satisfaction in the devil's service, if ever to one moment he could say, "Stay, thou art so fair," then all would be lost. But he never reached that depth. Though a slave, he could never bring himself to be satisfied with his slavery. That was his salvation. Had the prodigal been as satisfied with the husks as the hogs to which he ministered, he would not have risen above the hogs, but would have sunk below them.

What then, I repeat, does this prophet have to say to those who are seeking a satisfaction that they have never found? He tells them they can find what they seek only by finding God. Gripped by this conviction, Isaiah seems to rush in front of the restless, milling crowd, crying almost frantically, "Ho, everyone that thirsteth, come ye to the waters. Listen to me, incline your ear. The springs from which you are drinking can never slake your thirst. The bread that you are buying has no food value. You can only be satisfied by the Bread of Life and the Water of Life." His appeal is close akin to that made by Jesus himself centuries later when he shouted to the crowds about him: "If any man thirst, let him come unto me, and drink." The satisfaction that men seek can be found only in God.

In the grip of this faith the prophet continued his appeal, "Seek ye the Lord while he may be found, call ye upon him while he is near: let the wicked forsake his way, and the unrighteous man his thoughts: and let him return unto the Lord, and he will have mercy upon him; and to our God, for he will abundantly pardon." Pardon means something far bigger than the remission of a penalty. It means the restoration of a broken fellowship. It means that man need not be alone any longer, but that he may henceforth walk with God.

Not only does the prophet tell us that we can find in God the satisfaction for our hunger and thirst, the satisfaction of our longing for companionship; we can find here also satisfaction of our longing for usefulness. Every normal soul longs to be useful. The realization of this longing is made possible for those who accept the prophet's invitation. When we come to the waters for ourselves, we find not only personal satisfaction but something to share. "He that believeth on me, . . . from within him shall flow rivers of living water." God satisfies our longing for usefulness.

Then, too, as we give him opportunity, he satisfies our longing for joy. Every man who finds God, finds gladness. "The mountains and the hills," says this poet, "shall break forth before you into singing, and all the trees of the field shall clap their hands." Real joy does not come from the outside to make us glad within; it rather goes from within to transfigure what is without. Thackeray was right in saying: "We see the world with our own eyes, each of us, and make from within the world we see." The very hills sing for the man who has a song in his heart. To the wretched they only wail.

Finally, this great God of the prophet satisfies our hunger for life. "Hear," he pleads, "and your soul shall live." In God's presence life in the here and now becomes so rich and radiant that we yearn for an eternity of it. Are you satisfied? If not, you can find satisfaction by finding God. This does not mean, of course, that the God-conscious man has reached a goal beyond which there can be no more progress. He is satisfied, not simply because of what he has found today, but because of what he is sure he will go on finding tomorrow and tomorrow.

III

Is this declaration of the prophet that we find satisfaction in God true or false? Is it something that a modern man may believe without throwing dust in the eyes of reason and spitting in the face of common sense? I am convinced that the prophet is right for a number of reasons. I mention these among them:

1. His declaration of the adequacy of God for the satisfying of our hearts is not unique. It is the claim of the Bible as a whole. I am not asserting, mark you, that because the Bible makes such claim that claim is necessarily true. But I do affirm that the fact that this sanest of books makes such an assertion ought to predispose us in its favor. The writers of the Bible agree with the psalmist in saying, "He satisfieth the longing soul."

2. This is the verdict not only of the sunny saints whom we meet on the pages of the Bible, but also of those whom we meet ouside its pages. I am not here talking about the halfhearted; I am not here talking about nominal church members; I am speaking rather of those who have made a wholehearted committal of themselves to God. And this I say with boldness: I have yet to meet one who had made such committal who failed to convince me that he had found One who could satisfy both for time and for eternity. To the testimony of those, some of us can add our own experiences. Mine has been a faulty life. Countless times, I fear, my own shoddiness has contradicted the beautiful faith that I preach. Yet, this I say in all humility: Whenever I have given my Lord a chance, I, too, have found that he satisfies the longing soul.

3. Finally, I can believe this because it is so reasonable. One said of a happily married couple recently that they were meant for each other, that this marriage was really made in heaven. Maybe so, but in an infinitely profounder sense that is true of the relationship between God and man.

God has made us for himself. He made us for his fellowship, for the doing of his will. Life, therefore, will work that way, and it will not work any other. At Christmastime years ago we bought our small boys a lovely baby victrola. One day when Bob had heard its songs till he was weary, he decided to see how well it could play in reverse. But he never found out. He only wrecked the machine. It was not made to work that way. No more can you work satisfactorily except in accordance with the will of God.

Last summer it was my privilege to fish from a canoe on the waters of the Buffalo River. That canoe might have been used as a sled, or it might have been used as a swill trough to feed pigs. Had it been so used, it would not have been entirely wasted, though it would have been only an ugly bit of prose. But when it floated upon the clear waters of the river, it was not only useful; it became a veritable poem. An airship might be used for ground work. It can run on the ground, and swiftly at that. But it never comes to its best till it realizes its purpose by spurning the earth for the upper air.

Some time ago I took time to visit the zoo. There were some prisoners there for which I felt no pity. But when I looked at a great eagle, it was different. There he sat with his burnished brown wings draped slovenly about him like an ill-fitting old coat for which he had a contempt. That eagle was still alive, but for him the zoo offered a tame, drab life. Such an existence might have been satisfactory for a clucking hen. But to a great bird that was made to bathe his plumage in thunder's home, such an existence was thoroughly disappointing. We too are made for the heavenly places in Christ Jesus. We find where we fit in only when we find God.

Are you satisfied? If not, will you resolve here and now to quit spending "money for that which is not bread, and your labor for that which satisfieth not"? But some of you may answer, "I have spent so much for things that do not satisfy that I have little left for life's real values." In that case you are just the one to whom God is speaking. His appeal is to those who have no money. He offers his all to the spiritually impoverished who have nothing to give in return but their sinful selves. He is not a merchant who sells; he is a King who gives. "The gift of God is eternal life." Will you receive the gift?

> "Could my tears for ever flow,
>   Could my zeal no languor know,
>   These for sin could not atone;
>   Thou must save, and thou alone:
>   In my hand no price I bring;
>   Simply to thy cross I cling."

XVI

THE FIRST ELDER SON—JONAH

"That was why I fled."

JONAH 4:2 (Moffatt)

THE BOOK OF JONAH MUST HAVE BEEN VERY DEAR TO the heart of Jesus. So much was this the case that either consciously or unconsciously he created a character that is a blood brother to Jonah himself. Of all the men whom we meet upon the pages of the Bible, Jonah and the elder son are to my mind most alike. They were both upright men. They were both earnestly religious. They were both cold as icicles and hard as nails. They both made religion so unattractive that we are less repelled by the wickedness of the wicked than by the ugliness of such saints.

The story of Jonah is one of the amazingly beautiful miracles of the Old Testament. It is so fragrant with the breath of inspiration that it is impossible to account for it except in terms of God. To encounter such a roomy book in such a narrow age is a delicious thrill. It is like coming upon a garden sweet with perfume and colorful with flowers in the dreary hush of midwinter. In no other books of the Old Testament are narrowness, intolerance, selfishness more sharply rebuked. In no other book do we realize more compellingly the tender love of God, not only for all his children, but for all his creatures as well. Here we see that God cannot bear the thought of destroying Nineveh, not only because there are sixscore thousand babies within its walls, but also because there is much cattle. We cannot read this book without realizing that as God's children we must be brotherly toward all men. Not only so, but we must not be needlessly unkind to any living thing. Coleridge had the idea when he sang:

> "He prayeth best, who lovest best
> All things both great and small;
> For the dear God who loveth us,
> He made and loveth all."

How tragic, therefore, that often we have argued so hotly over the queer garb in which this mesage comes to us that we have forgotten the message itself! There is a story of two men who lost their way in a desert. When their tongues were swollen with thirst and they felt themselves doomed to die, they came upon a bottle of water that someone who had passed their way had either left or lost. At first they welcomed this boon as a gift from God's own hand. But before they had tasted a drop of the water, they noticed that the bottle was of queer and unusual shape. The two starving men became so excited and indignant as they argued about the queerness of the bottle that they spilled all the water into the desert sands. Thus have we sometimes lost the life-giving water contained in this book. So much is this the case that it is hard today to mention the name of Jonah without provoking a smile. Thus we have taken one who was sent as a messenger of God and have made him into a creature close akin to a clown. Again I say, how tragic!

Is the story of Jonah true? Indeed it is. It is true as the story of the elder son is true. Though Jonah is a historical character, that does not mean that this episode in his life is factual. Why? Because God could not create a fish that could swallow a man? By no means. To make such a contention would be as silly as arguing over whether a man who had just lifted a mountain could lift a bit of thistledown. Of course God could create such a fish. That would certainly be no chore for him who dipped his hand into the chalice of the eternities and made the oceans to drip and the rivers to flow. The impossibility of the story is that a great city could repent in sackcloth and ashes and yet remain just the same as it was before this transforming experience. If Nineveh literally repented, nobody ever found it out but the author of this book. For the plain truth is that Nineveh lived out its bloody, greedy, despotic days and died at last of its own iniquities. Let us then forget what is incidental in this great story and look to what is fundamental.

I

The first truth that impresses us is that to this man Jonah came a definite and specific call from God. That call was this: "Arise, go to Nineveh, that great city, and cry against it." How this call came we do not know. Of this we may be sure, that God called Jonah just as he calls men today. He may have called through Jonah's consciousness of the needs of Nineveh. He may have called through the voice of the Holy Spirit. But however the voice came, Jonah was sure of its meaning and authority, far too sure for his own comfort.

Not only did God call Jonah to a definite task, but with an engaging frankness he gave his reasons for so calling him. Jonah was to go to Nineveh and cry against it, not because the inhabitants of Nineveh were not Jews. God's objection to Nineveh was not that it was outside the covenant. His objection to Nineveh was that it was outside his holy will. He was sending a prophet to Nineveh because it was a wicked city and therefore needed to turn from its wickedness to God.

Then he was sending his prophet to Nineveh not only because Nineveh was wicked, but because, in spite of its wickedness, it was a great city. It was great in the number of its inhabitants, great in its need, great in its suffering, great in its possibilities. God was so concerned for this great and wicked city because the people of Nineveh were his children and because, since they were his children, he loved every soul that dwelt within its walls. This call was doubtless a great shock to Jonah. It was certainly vastly unwelcome. The last thing that this strait-laced prophet desired to do was to go as a missionary to Nineveh.

But he did not shrink from this task for ordinary reasons. For instance, he did not shrink from it because of the labor that such an adventure would require. He does not seem to have minded work. No more did the elder son.

"Now his elder son was in the field." He was out where the sun blazed hot. He was out where the soil was to be turned, where the seed were to be sown, where the crop was to be cultivated, where the harvest was to be gathered. These were both willing enough to work provided the work was to their liking.

No more did Jonah shrink from this task because he believed that it would be futile to preach to the people of Nineveh. It never occurred to him that they were of such a low order that they had no capacity to respond to God. Some of us have friends to whom we refuse to speak because we have convinced ourselves that it would do no good. When Darwin visited Terra del Fuego, he declared that the inhabitants were so low that they were incapable of being civilized. But when he visited those inhabitants years later, he found that they had become not only civilized but Christian. For this reason he was ever after that a contributor to missions. Jonah did not refuse this mission because he was convinced that it was foredoomed to failure.

If Jonah was not afraid of the work or of failure, of what was he afraid? He was afraid of success. He was afraid that the people of Nineveh would repent. He was afraid that thus repenting they would become as dear to the heart of God as he and his fellow Jews. That, he felt, would be disastrous. That would make futile the prayer that he had prayed all his life, that every Jewish boy prayed: "Thank God I was not born a Gentile, a leper, or a woman." He was sure that in building up the people of Nineveh he would be tearing down his own people. He was equally sure that in tearing others down he was building up himself and his own. A thoroughly stupid faith, but one that takes a long time in dying.

Now this clear call demanded some kind of action. Jonah had either to obey or disobey, even as you and I. He decided to disobey. We read that he rose up to flee to Tarshish from the presence of the Lord. But it was not the Lord he was really seeking to escape. He was rather seeking to escape the Lord's troublesome children. He saw that if he continued to claim God as his Father, he must recognize all God's children as his brothers, even the people of Nineveh. He was so unwilling to do this that he decided rather than accept both God and his children he would renounce both. That same decision confronts every man. Jonah had no special objection to God, but he did object most strenuously to some of God's children. And yet no man can have God without taking the attitude of a brother to every child of God.

Some time ago a husband who was having more difficulty with his "inlaws" than he knew how to manage said indignantly: "But I did not marry the whole family. I just married Mary." Well, he discovered his mistake when his mother-in-law came to spend the winter with him. Generally speaking, when we marry Mary we have in some measure to marry Mary's family. Always when we claim God as our Father we have to take the attitude of brother toward his children. God can no more accept as his child one who hates his brother than he can make twice two equal five. To accept God is to accept brotherhood. To deny brotherhood is to deny God. If we love not our brother whom we have seen, how can we love God whom we have not seen? Thus facing all the issues involved, called to go in the direction of brotherhood, Jonah went in the opposite direction.

II

Now in spite of his rebellion God gave Jonah a second chance. How did it come about?

When Jonah made up his mind to flee to Tarshish, he went on shipboard and down into the hull of the vessel, where he went fast asleep. This story is psychologically sound. It had cost Jonah a severe struggle to renounce God. The days and nights preceding his flight had been full of agony. There are few things more torturing than indecision. While a wrong decision never brings rest, it comes nearer to it than no decision at all. Having decided to renounce all claim on God, the prophet went into a profound sleep. This was his period of greatest danger. Even though he had been a rebel before, he had at least been a restless and wretched rebel. Now he is not only a rebel; he has found a measure of contentment in his rebellion.

But God never allows us to wreck ourselves by our foolish rebellion without doing his infinite best to save us. This he did for Jonah. The vessel on which the sleeping prophet was sailing was no more than out of port before God hurled a great storm into the sea. We may be thankful that the rebel's voyage is never over entirely smooth seas. In some fashion God always tells us that we are headed in the wrong direction. It was through this storm and through the ministry of pagan hands that Jonah was awakened.

While the tempest was raging, the ship's captain gripped the sleeping prophet by the shoulder and shouted: "What meanest thou, O sleeper? arise, call upon thy God."

Once awake, Jonah hurried on deck, where he was made to see that he and the pagans were all in the same boat. They were threatened by a common disaster. They were a part, as Wendell Willkie said, of "one world." Being thus bound together in a bundle of life with others, Jonah discovered that his wrongdoing had hurt these pagans whose faces he had never seen. He could not fail to realize also that by his "rightdoing" he could help. The plain truth is no man ever goes wrong alone, just as no man ever goes right alone. If we take the downward trail, somebody will follow us into the depths. If we take the upward way, somebody will climb to where the light lingers even when the sun is set.

When those on board had cast lots to discover who was responsible and the lot had fallen on Jonah, he did the one decent thing that the author attributes to him. Seeing that if they continued as they were, all would perish, he decided to be thrown into the sea in order to save the innocent victims of his disobedience. But though his fellow voyagers were sure of his guilt, they did their best to save him. "The men dug in their oars," says the author, "to row the ship to land." But when they realized the futility of it all, that they were fighting against God, they cast Jonah into the sea. A great fish furnished him his transportation to the land. Then at last the reluctant prophet accepted his mission.

III

What was the final outcome? Though Jonah went upon the mission to which he had been called, it is quite evident that he did not do so in the spirit of a son, but in the spirit of a slave. He had no love for God or for God's children. Here again he reminds us of the elder son. He, too, was an obedient worker. Listen to him: "Look at all the years I have been serving you! I never neglected any of your orders." But there was no love in his service either to his father or to his brother. Both of these were obedient, but theirs was the obedience of slaves rather than of sons.

Arrived at Nineveh, Jonah went a day's journey into the city and began to proclaim his message: "Yet forty days, and Nineveh shall be overthrown." Now God's warnings are always conditional, just as are his promises. God promises the gift of himself, the Holy Spirit, to every one of us, but only on the condition that we obey him. This condition is not arbitrary. It exists in the very nature of things. Two cannot walk together except they be agreed. God's warnings are also conditional. These people were to perish if they refused to repent. Of course, the moment they ceased to rebel against God, he was ready to become their friend.

Having delivered his message, Jonah retired to what amounted to a ringside seat to witness the destruction which he had prophesied and for which he longed. I can imagine that soon there were shouts in the streets of the city. Jonah listened hopefully. Then he discovered that these shouts were not the terrified shouts of those who were being destroyed, but the joyful shouts of those who through repentance were finding salvation. Then what? Did he rejoice over an event that must have thrilled all heaven? By no means. He only became angry. "That was why I fled," he complains. "I knew thou wert a gracious and pitiful God, slow to be angry, rich in love, and ready to relent!"

That has a familiar ring, does it not? Listen to this: "Now his elder son was in the field: and he came and drew nigh to the house, he heard music and dancing. And he called one of the servants, and asked what these things meant. And he said unto him Thy brother is come; and thy father hath killed the fatted calf, because he hath received him safe and sound. And he was angry, and would not go in." When the prodigal city repented, Jonah was angry just as the elder son when the prodigal came home.

What lay back of this anger? Proud, pharisaical selfishness. These two religious men were not guilty of the sins of the swine pen. Theirs were the sins of the disposition, the sins of those who thank God that they are not as other men. Did the repentance of Nineveh rob Jonah of anything? Did the return of the prodigal cheat his elder brother? By no means. Why then were they angry? Their anger was born of their envy. They felt that the good to another was a hurt to themselves. Thus what should have made them vastly richer only added to their spiritual povety.

In my opinion this envy that tortured these two is not to be confused with jealousy. As a certain English author affirms, jealousy is a child of love. It is an emotion that love feels when it is cheated of its dues. I know that often it is the green-eyed monster that makes the meat it feeds upon. But sometimes that meat is made by another. In that case jealousy is normal, if not inevitable. But envy is always a deadly evil. It is a child of selfishness. It homes in the heart of him who hates. It is that vile something that makes us suffer in another's good and rejoice in another's evil. It was born with a murderous club in its hand, and it has been a murderer ever since.

Did Jonah ever repent? Did he ever come to see through God's eyes and to share in God's compassion? We do not know any more than we know about the repentance of the elder son. The last glimpse we get of Jonah he is red-faced with anger, partly because of the mercies of God to others and partly because of a small personal loss to himself. So far as the story goes, he never learns to love. The nearest he approaches to it is his care for a vine that has sheltered him. Even so, the last glimpse we get of the elder son, he is shutting the door to the feast in his own face, because he had rather miss that feast than to enjoy it as the brother of a prodigal. So may we fail in our time. For there is simply no door to the feast of the fullness of life unless we are willing to enter as a brother to every other guest.

XVII

MASTERING OUR DIFFICULTIES —ZECHARIAH

"Who art thou, O great mountain? before Zerubbabel thou shalt become a plain."

ZECHARIAH 4:7

ZECHARIAH HAD RETURNED WITH HIS FELLOW EXILES to rebuild the city of Jerusalem and its ruined temple. They had set out on their enterprise with high hopes. They were undergirded by great expectations. They were sure that under the guidance of God their city and temple were soon to be restored to their old-time splendor. But in this they were doomed to disappointment. They found themselves, as time went on, confronted by stubborn difficulties that seemed to make the realization of their dreams impossible. For this reason many were disappointed and discouraged. Some were embittered and ready to give up the enterprise altogether.

Now it was to this disappointed and disillusioned people that Zechariah was sent. He seems to have been raised up of God to speak a word of encouragement to a group that had become thoroughly discouraged. He was sent to relight the candle of hope and expectancy in lives where the light had gone out. His was therefore a great mission. Of all the benefactors who help us in the business of living, few, I think, are so helpful as those who have skill to put heart into the hopeless and to change sobs into songs. This young prophet did not shut his eyes to the difficulties, but he faced them in the light of God. Thus facing them, he uttered this heartening word: "Who art thou, O great mountain? before Zerubbabel thou shalt become a plain."

I

We need this word today because we, too, are confronted by difficulties.

1. We have our international difficulties. The millions all round the world are eager for abiding peace. They long for a sense of security. Will a good day ever come when men shall beat their swords into plowshares and their spears into pruning hooks and learn war no more? Everybody longs for such a day. Too few expect it. This is the case because difficulties mountain high seem to block the road that leads to permanent world peace. Thus we have our international difficulties.

2. Then we have our difficulties as a nation. At this moment capital and labor are wasting millions as they war with each other. In this mad battle for supremacy there is too little indication of any unselfish desire for the common good. Each seems bent on mastering the other without the least regard for those who belong to neither of these groups. In such an affirmation of "every fellow for himself and the devil take the hindmost," the devil threat-

ens to get the foremost as well. We are confronted today by grim national problems.

3. Then we have our problems as a church. It is my conviction that of all churches the most important is the downtown city church. It stands "where cross the crowded ways of life." It stands amidst the city traffic proclaiming by its very presence that man shall not live by bread alone. It is to the city somewhat as the heart is to the human body. If it is strong and vigorous, it helps every other church in the city. If it becomes weak and faltering, it weakens every other church.

As the downtown church is of all others the most necessary, even so it is the most difficult. This is the case for many reasons. In the first place, it is a church without a parish. The whole city must be its parish. Therefore, many of its members live in the very shadow of strong suburban churches. If they have children, often the children go to this near-by church to Sunday school. By and by they join and take their parents with them. Thus the downtown church is constantly giving members to suburban churches. Since it is thus constantly giving, it must be constantly receiving. This it must do to a greater degree than other churches by capturing from without instead of nurturing from within. The suburban church can often keep alive by the members received from its church school. Such is not generally the case with a downtown church. This church must be aggressively evangelistic or die.

To conquer as it should, the downtown church must have more than one victorious Sunday service. The suburban church may live on one service a week, but not the downtown church. It must have not only a morning service but an evening service as well. This has increased its difficulties. Evening services have gone out of style. The modern Christian is, generally speaking, too delicate to face the night air. In spite of these difficulties, not a few downtown churches are going from victory to victory; but many are sickly, and some have died. We face our difficulties as a church.

4. Then we have our individual difficulties. Some are looking with eyes full of foreboding at the mountains that seem to block the path ahead. For some it is an economic difficulty. They are facing a prospect of want where once there was wealth. For others it is some personal loss, the blighting of some hope, or the death of some dear dream. For others still it is a domestic tragedy that has hung crape, not upon the doors of their homes, but upon the doors of their hearts. Then there are others still to whom the mountain is some handicap which seems like a ball and chain about their ankles. For others still it is the seeming impossibility of being what they long to be or doing what they long to do. We have our individual difficulties.

II

What are we going to do about these difficulties? When our road comes up against some forbidding mountain, we do not all react in the same fashion.

1. For instance, some ignore the mountain, shut their eyes to it altogether. This is a very real remedy provided the mountain is not a reality. Often that is the case. Physicians tell us that more than half of the patients who occupy

beds in our hospitals are suffering from diseases of the mind rather than of the body. An imaginary pain is just as tormenting as a real pain. The only difference is that, generally speaking, it is harder to cure. Imaginary difficulties ought to be ignored.

But if ignoring is a real remedy for imaginary evils, it is equally true that such a course is an imaginary remedy for evils that are real. The majority of the accidents that befall our commercial planes come about because pilots fly into the side of a mountain. The pilot may be quite sure that there is no mountain there; but, if he is mistaken, the wreck is just as fatal as if he had known of its existence all along. When I started for the door the other night, I was sure there was no obstruction in my way, but the fact that I was sure did not save me from the barked shin that resulted from my running into a chair. Therefore, we cannot master our real mountains by simply shutting our eyes.

2. There is a second group, who, coming up against a mountain, refuse either to level it with the ground or to scale it. They seek an easy way round it. They believe that the supreme purpose of life should be to find not character but comfort. When they stand at the forks of the road, they do not ask which turn leads to their desired goal, but which so avoids all mountains as to be easy to travel. These are determined to live on Easy Street even though that street may end in Rotten Row.

But to make ease the test of conduct is surely to make a tragic mess of the business of living. Jeroboam wrecked a whole nation in that fashion. When he became king of the ten tribes he realized that, while the Israelites were divided politically, they were still one religiously. He was afraid that, if they continued to be one in religion, they would soon become one politically. Therefore, he set about the task of dividing them religiously. How did he go about it? He did not tell them that their religion was wrong. He told them that it was too costly, that they could get by at far less expense. This was his word: "It is too much for you to go up to Jerusalem." To demand an easy way out of a hard situation is a sure road to failure.

3. There are others who go bravely forward until their smooth road seems to come to a dead end against some mountain; then they make an abject surrender. Sometimes these fall in self-pity and wail bitterly: "Why should this happen to me?" But whether in cowardly self-pity or in bitterness, they tell themselves that the mountain can neither be made into a plain or scaled. Thus they accept defeat as final and complete.

During my first year in the ministry I was moved from a country circuit to a church in the city. It so happened that the pastor whose place I took was very popular. For this reason the congregation blamed his elder for moving him. They blamed him for going. They blamed me for coming. But, since I was the only man on the field, all three blames fell on me. At my first appearance in the pulpit two sisters sitting in the front pew gave me one glance and then burst into tears. Even after the wonderful sermon that I preached, the atmosphere did not greatly change. A few days later one came with the encouraging news that Mr. X was going to quit the church. "Why?" I questioned. "Because you are not big enough to fill the place, and he is not going to stand by and have the church fall about his ears," was the candid and kindly answer.

Some six weeks later, after I had heard other words equally encouraging, I came into the pulpit one morning, held up a sheaf of paper, and said: "See this? It is paper for the writing of church certificates. I saw something this week," I continued, "that encouraged me greatly. I watched a man buy a bottle of soda pop. When" (according to the custom of some thirty-five years ago) "he knocked the stopper in, it began to splutter and boil as if the last drop of it were going to escape. I could hardly keep from shouting at the stranger, 'Drink it, man, drink it! You will lose it all.' But the reckless spendthrift waited until it had lapsed into silence. Then I looked and could hardly credit what I saw. For, believe it or not, the bottle seemed as full as it was at the beginning. Nothing had escaped but a few bubbles." So I said, "You who have been bubbling, come and get your letters." Nobody came. Yet there are always those who fall in abject surrender before a real difficulty.

4. Then there is a fourth group who neither shut their eyes, nor demand an easy way, nor surrender. They defy their mountains and either level them with the plains or climb over them. This was a posibility ahead of the discouraged people to whom Zechariah spoke. It is a posibility for you and me. This is a word for every one of us. "Who art thou, O mountain? before me thou shalt become a plain."

III

How shall we thus master our mountains?

1. In winning such a victory it would help us to realize

that the mountains we face are not altogether unique. Perhaps you feel that nobody else ever confronted such ugly difficulties as you must meet. But difficulties are incidental to the business of living. Life, if it is of any worth at all, is a conflict. This is especially true of the Christian life. If you have made up your mind to be a follower of Jesus Christ, you had better make up your mind to fight and to fight gallantly. Jesus was eager for followers, but he never once appealed to any man's loyalty on the basis that such loyalty would cost him nothing. Jesus knew that to follow him was surely to get into trouble.

For instance, when one came asking: "Are there few that be saved?" Jesus did not give the desired answer. He did not say whether there would be many or few. Instead he said: "Strive to enter in at the strait gate." Strive —that is a word wet with sweat and flecked with blood. It is a muscular, battling word. It means fight to enter in, agonize somewhat, as Jesus agonized in Gethsemane, to enter in. If you are finding life a fight, it is nothing more than what it is to be expected. If you are escaping all conflict, you had better look well to your guideposts; for the chances are that you are on the wrong road.

2. It will help also to remember that the difficulties confronting us are one big reason for our being here. I put some work and much hope into a certain meeting years ago. I invited an able man whom I held in peculiar honor to be the speaker. I expected hundreds if not thousands to come to hear his one address, but a mere handful came. The failure depressed me even while it made me indignant.

I apologized to the great man whom I had invited—whined a bit, perhaps. Anyway he gave this fine answer: "My son, if everybody were just as interested in the good as they ought to be, the Lord would not need you and me. Because they are not, that is the reason we are here."

Do you find yourself up against difficulties which loom so large that they seem stark impossibilities? That means that yours is a place of peculiar honor. You have come to the kingdom for such a time as this. Therefore, instead of whining, instead of pitying yourself, instead of telling yourself that nothing can be done about it, rather thank God that he can trust you enough to match you against these mighty mountains. For believe me, these forbidding mountains are one big reason for your being where you are.

3. It will help us further to bear in mind that there is no difficulty that can wreak our final defeat. Instead, we can make every single opposition minister to our enrichment. Paul found this true so many times that he reached a definite conclusion. "We know," he declared, "that all things work together for good to them that love God." This is true of the road that stretches away in level distances. It is equally true of the road that winds over rugged mountains. In fact, when we look about us for those who have lived most richly, we find that they are not sheltered souls for whom life has been easy. They are rather those whose road has been blocked by one forbidding mountain after another. Every difficulty, therefore, may add to our enrichment.

4. Finally, if we change our mountains into plains or if we are to scale them as if they were level ground, we must

approach them undergirded by a vital faith in God. He alone is our adequacy for meeting life's impossibilities. Jesus perhaps had this word of the prophet in mind when he declared that everyone whose faith is real can toss mountains about as a juggler tosses a ball.

It is through faith in God that we achieve the impossible within ourselves. Our Lord is constantly calling us to what in our own strength we cannot accomplish. One day he looked into the face of a man who had been flat on his back for thirty-eight years. He commanded this man to do the impossible. "Rise, take up thy bed, and walk." But as he willed what Jesus willed for him, as he believed that he could do what was commanded, the impossible became possible; and he rose and walked. To be new creations in Christ Jesus, to love our neighbors as we love ourselves— these are big impossibilities that become possible only through faith in God.

Not only do we become the impossible through faith, but we also accomplish the impossible. The writer to the Hebrews calls attention to the fact that, although the Egyptians and Hebrews went down the same road, encountered the same impassable barrier, the Red Sea, one found this barrier a terminus, the other found it a thoroughfare. One found it a way of death, and the other found it a way of life. Why the difference? It was not that this horde of Hebrew slaves was superior to the Egyptians. The difference was that the Hebrews had faith in God, while the others did not.

Had a friend pointed out that little handful of disciples who years ago went into the upper room where they experienced Pentecost and said to me: "These are going to remake the world. They are going to spread over this Roman Empire like a life-giving springtime. In their presence the flowers are going to bloom, and millions are going to be made conscious of God. By them the whole world is going to be changed"—had anyone spoken after that fashion, I should have said, "Impossible." In so saying I would have been entirely right. Yet it happened nonetheless. The same may be true for us. Therefore, I may dare to shout in the presence of the difficulties that confront me: "Who art thou, O great mountain? before me, as I approach you in the fellowship of God, thou shalt become a plain."

XVIII

BORED FOLKS—MALACHI

"What a weariness it all is!"

MALACHI 1:13 (Moffatt)

THE AUTHOR OF THE BOOK OF WHICH THESE WORDS are a part did not see fit to tell us his name. He describes himself, however, in a clear and graphic way. He is the messenger. He is God's spokesman. He was evidently a man of deep moral earnestness and of keen insight. He was called to speak to a very difficult congregation. It was a congregation that was not athrill with expectancy. Instead, it was bored, fed up, saying of life in general and of religion in particular: "What a weariness it all is!" These people of the long ago, as are so many today, were intensely bored.

I

Now boredom is not an asset. It is a heavy liability. This I say in spite of the fact that I have found a few sophisticated souls here and there who seem to think that being bored is one of the finest of the fine arts. There are those who pride themselves on never thrilling over anything. They have their emotions under perfect control. They seem to find a somber joy in being able to greet life's thrilling experiences with yawns. Yet to be proud of being bored is about as silly as pride in an incurable case of tuberculosis or a malignant cancer.

1. This is the case, in the first place, because boredom is a kill-joy. However rich the treasures that life may have spilled into your roomy hands, if you are bored, then all those treasures count for next to naked nothing. If you are bored, there is no blue in your sky, no brightness in your sunshine. Life for you is about as thrilling as a tomb and stuffy as a dust storm. To allow yourself to be bored is to allow yourself to be cheated of the joy of living.

2. Then boredom is a heavy liability because of the silly and hurtful things it often sets us to doing in an effort to escape its bondage. How much time and energy, for instance, we burn up trying to escape by the door of amusement! Now some form of recreation is both wholesome and necessary. If all work and no play makes Jack a dull boy, all work and no play is apt to make Jack's father a dead one. But multitudes today are not using amusements in such a fashion as to make them a recreation; they are so using them as to make of them a dissipation. Take a simple pastime like playing bridge, for instance. Playing bridge in itself may be as harmless as mumblety-peg. But it becomes a positive and deadly evil to some because they make it so nearly into a vocation. They thus change a recreation into dissipation in an effort to escape boredom.

But boredom has far uglier sins to its credit than this.

Why will the night clubs all over America be thronged tonight? Why will so many engage in those high-powered dances, whose supreme appeal is to the sexual? Why will otherwise decent and honest folks throng the gambling tables? Why will so many get drunk? It is not that they are all vicious scoundrels who are out to wreck themselves and their fellows. They are, generally speaking, ordinary people like ourselves. Through these varied types of dissipation they are simply seeking an escape from the dull, drab monotony of living.

3. Not only is boredom a kill-joy driving its victim often to foolish efforts to escape; but if prolonged it is slow or rapid suicide. "Many of my patients," said a physician some time ago to his minister, "are suffering from a disease that my medicine is powerless to reach."

"What is that?" asked the minister, thinking the physician might be speaking of some deadly malady like cancer.

"They are suffering from boredom," came the answer.

No doubt tens of thousands die every year from this deadly disease.

Here, for instance, is a man who has worked hard. He has never learned to play. He has no hobbies, not even the hobby of serving others. By and by he retires. Why should he work any longer? He has accumulated more than enough to live on for the rest of his days. But his real problem is not something to live on, but something to live for. Lacking that, life often becomes so stale and unpalatable that he dies of sheer boredom. In fact, this boredom often becomes so intense and painful that its victim flings his life away by his own hand. I was reading some time ago of a young chap of ability and education. Yet he had never found any large and thrilling interest outside of himself. He had never been gripped by a purpose that was big enough to command him. Therefore, he dared to quit before the whistle blew, giving as his reason that he was too bored to live.

4. Finally, boredom is bad not only for what it does to its possessor, but for what it causes him to do to others. If you live in a constant state of boredom, you are at best a pest and at worst a positive menace. Did you ever try to entertain anybody who simply refused to be entertained? I undertook to thrill a young lady by my conversation many years ago. But the most extravagant statement I was ever able to elicit from her was "You don't say." She kept repeating that until I felt like shrieking at her: "I do say! That's what I am positively sweating over right now." By and by I escaped from the wet blanket with the high resolve in my heart, Never again.

This tells why some men leave home. Think of going at the close of each day's work to meet a wife who has allowed herself to become an incarnate yawn. This tells why some women get old before their time. Spring soon gives place to winter if its luxurious life is constantly being nipped by the killing frost of a bored husband. Boredom, then, is an ugly liability that we ought to flee as we would flee a pestilence.

II

"What a weariness it all is!" How had these people got that way? How had they made of religion a weight instead of wings? It was not because they renounced religion altogether. They were bored because of the kind of religion they had come to possess. What kind was it?

1. They chose a cheap religion. A cheap religion always leads to dissatisfaction and boredom. In *The Screwtape Letters,* Screwtape, a seasoned old devil, is writing to a young kinsman of his, named Wormwood, who is engaged in seeking to wreck a certain man. He writes as follows: "I note that your patient has become religious. Do not let that disturb you so long as he is only moderately religious. Remember that religion in moderation is just as good for us as no religion at all, and far more amusing."

In cheapening their religion these people had not asked how much they could do, but how little. They were trying to get by on the least possible. When they offered a lamb in sacrifice, they did not offer the best in the flock, as they were commanded. They rather offered one that was sick and useless. In other words, they gave to God something that they did not wish for themselves. They also economized on their giving of money. They were commanded to tithe, but that seemed altogether too much. Therefore, they began to hold out on God. It was this cheapening of their gifts that had shut the windows of heaven above their heads. It was this cheapening of their service that little by little changed their religion from something that was thrilling into something that was monotonous and boring.

Then they had cheapened their religion in another way. They were seeking to make religious observances a substitute for right living. They had not left off attending church altogether. They had not left off saying prayers. They sometimes covered the altar of the Lord with their tears and their crying out, so the prophet tells us. But such religious performances were sheer futility and mockery. They were asking God to forgive them for sins they were not willing to give up. By their prayers they were seeking to win the privileges of sinning without having to pay the penalty. Therefore, though God's arm was not shortened that he could not save nor his ear heavy that he could not hear, their sin had made his help impossible.

The particular sin of which many of these were guilty was the sin of unfaithfulness to the marriage relationship. "I was a witness," God said, "when you married in your youth." Whoever else was at the wedding ceremony, when you or I married, God was there. He heard the vows we made. He is interested that those vows be kept. Divorce had become very easy then, as it has today. "I hate divorce," God said then, as he says today. No amount of praying, no amount of giving, no amount of religious observance is of any worth toward our salvation unless we are willing to give up our sin.

2. These people were bored with religion because theirs was a religion of self-pleasing. Naturally they desired to please themselves without displeasing God, but the desire to please self was central. Now self-pleasing always leads to boredom. It is one of the surest of all sure roads. Here, for instance, is a child whose will is never crossed, whose every whim is gratified. Such a child is never happy. It is always fretful and peevish and bored. I am thinking now of a couple who said of their promising son that he was too fine to be curbed. From his very infancy, therefore, all roads led to Rome; and he was Rome. By and by they had

to employ a strong Negro man whose one duty it was to amuse him from the time he awoke in the morning until he went to sleep at night. His toys were not quite numerous enough to have filled the toy departments of Sears Roebuck and Montgomery Ward combined. But in spite of the constant effort made for his amusement, his brows were puckered into a persistent frown. He would have been far happier with a goose-quill whistle plus some genuine discipline than he was with all his treasures without discipline.

Just as self-pleasing leads to boredom for a child, so it does for the adult. If you have nothing to do but to live your own life, then that life is as dull as a yawn. A brilliant young chap who went through a well-known university was dedicated by his parents to the ministry. But when he reached his majority he said: "I have been doing to please the old folks. I am now going to please myself." So what? He did not go to the dogs and the devil. He became a physician, and a most excellent and successful one. Yet when he was in his middle thirties, he wrote a letter that was a classic. In this letter he declared: "I am clean tired of doing as I please. I long to bathe my weary soul in the ether of eternity." He then put a gun to his temple and ended it all. A religion of self-pleasing must end in boredom.

3. Then these people were bored not only because they were self-centered but because their self-centeredness had robbed them of their usefulness. They had lost the thrill of being a blessing. "Your words have been stout against me," God is represented as saying to them. When, in amazement, they asked what they had said against God, he

answered, "Ye have said, it is vain to serve God." In other words, you have declared that there is really nothing in religion—that it is a dull, futile, boring thing with which nobody would have to do except fear. Thus they had slandered God and had turned others from religion by making it ugly.

Now, of course, we are not to assume that these people had openly declared that religion was a boring and secondary matter. At least they had not said such ugly words with their lips. But they had said them in a more impressive way, and that is with their lives. How often we cheapen our religion and make it contemptible in the eyes of our children without any thought of doing so! For instance, last Sunday morning it was a bit gloomy. There was some rain, not a big rain, just a little baby rain. But when you looked out, you resolved that you would not expose either yourself or your children to such horrible weather. You could not risk your life by venturing out to church; therefore, you stayed at home in snug safety.

Then came Monday morning. The clouds had not cleared. They had grown thicker and blacker. The rain had not lessened. Instead it had grown from a mere pygmy into a giant. So what? Did you again stay home and keep snug and warm? No, you went to business as usual. Every chick and child went to school. Thus you said to your child: "My dear, it is all right to be religious so long as your religion dosen't cost you anything in particular. But never make it central in your life." This was your way of saying that it is vain to serve the Lord. It was also your way of missing your chance of finding and being a blessing.

4. Thus refusing to obey God, thus cheating themselves of the joy of service, these people passed inevitably to the supreme cause of boredom, which is a lost sense of God. Every man who is bored with religion is bored not because of what he knows, but because of what he does not know. There are few things more deadly boring than a form of godliness without the power. To fail to know God is to find religion a very dull and drab affair. This is the case because ignorance is a fruitful cause of boredom everywhere.

Some years ago I went to hear one of the greatest living concert pianists. It so happened I had to take my small boy who was about four years of age. We sat together through three long, difficult numbers. Then the boy looked up and said: "Daddy, let's go. That old man ain't doing nothing." Hand in hand we left. Some of my musical friends looked after me with pity and whispered: "His little boy is making him leave." Well, the little boy helped, but to be perfectly honest I was not getting much more out of it than the small boy. This was the case, not because of my knowledge, but because of my ignorance. These people had come to boredom because in spite of religious observances they had failed to know God.

III

How shall we escape boredom?

Well, we are not likely to escape by the winning of things. The author of the book of Ecclesiastes called himself "The Preacher." This preacher was immensely rich. He was rich in things. He was rich in achievement. He was a great builder. He was rich in intellectual ability. But he was the most bored man of his day. All nature was for him a mere treadmill. Man was a futile creature. Being a bit loyal to his own sex, he thought such a thing as a good man might possibly be found, but a good woman was simply out of the question. Not only so, but the crooked could never be made straight. Because life was purposeless and without meaning, in spite of all its possessions he was utterly bored. The best he could say for life was: "Vanity of vanities, . . . all is vanity." How then, I repeat, shall we escape boredom?

1. If we are to escape boredom, we must keep up our interest in others. Once begin to live solely for self, and life will lose its tang. Here is one of the finest characters of the Old Testament. His name is Caleb. He is now past eighty. Everybody says that he ought to retire. But, instead, he comes at the late eventide of life to ask for the hardest job that he has ever had. How much he accomplished for his people by his adventure we do not know. But of this we may be sure: by thus keeping up interest he found life thrilling to the very end.

2. If we are to escape boredom, we must have a satisfying religion. For this reason the prophet urges his own people to repentance. They are to give up their evil ways and turn back to God in wholehearted consecration. By so doing they will find God, and finding him they will find One in whose presence life never grows stale. Real saints are never among the bored and fed-up. Years ago when one sought to explain the thrill of those participating in Pentecost, he declared that they were filled with new wine.

This was the wine of God's giving. Its intoxication lasts. It never leaves us, as does other wine, with an ill head and an aching heart. I have known consecrated people in vastly different circumstances. Some were young, some were old, some were rich, some were poor, some were strong in body, and some were on beds of pain. But I have yet to hear one real Christian say: "What a weariness it all is!" The sure way, therefore, to escape boredom and to find life thrilling is to dedicate life to God.